Outline Studies in the New Testament for Bible Teachers

Outline Studies in the New Testament for Bible Teachers

by Jesse Lyman Hurlbut

Contents

PREFATORY 4

HINTS TO STUDENTS 6

HINTS TO TEACHERS 7

THE COURSE DIVIDED INTO LESSONS 8

FIRST STUDY...9

SECOND STUDY 15

THIRD STUDY 20

FOURTH STUDY...25

    From the Birth of Jesus to His Temptation. 25

FIFTH STUDY 29

    From the First Followers of Jesus to His Return to Galilee. 29

SIXTH STUDY 33

    From the Rejection at Nazareth to the Discourse on the Bread of Life 33

SEVENTH STUDY...40

    From the Retirement to Phœnicia to the Anointing by Mary.........40

EIGHTH STUDY 45

    From the Triumphal Entry Until the Agony in the Garden..............45

NINTH STUDY..49

    From the Betrayal to the Burial of Jesus...49

TENTH STUDY..54

    From the Resurrection to the Ascension of Christ........................54

ELEVENTH STUDY...57

TWELFTH STUDY 61

THIRTEENTH STUDY 64

FOURTEENTH STUDY...70

   From the Appointment of the Seven, A. D. 35, to the Council at Jerusalem, A. D. 50. 70

FIFTEENTH STUDY 75

SIXTEENTH STUDY..78

SEVENTEENTH STUDY 84

   From the Council at Jerusalem, A. D. 50, To the Death of St. Paul, A. D. 68...84

EIGHTEENTH STUDY..91

   From the Death of St. Paul, A. D. 68, to the Death of St. John, 100 A. D...91

PREFATORY

There is no book in the world which repays earnest study so abundantly as the Holy Bible. Even the cursory reader who possesses a candid mind can gather many precious thoughts from its pages; and he who turns to it for guidance in life, however ignorant he may be, will never be led astray. But as the precious metal lies hidden in the mountains, and must be sought out by the miners, so the treasures in the Word of Life are found only by those who search diligently for them. He who not only reads but *studies* the Scriptures finds an abundant reward. There is need in our age of searchers in the Bible, who shall bring out of its treasure-house things new and old.

In the old Bible the most important themes are those which gather around the God-man, Jesus Christ. His coming to earth was the culmination of all prophecy, the focus of all history, and the center of all doctrine; and the church which he founded has been for nineteen centuries the inspiration of the world's progress. There are two subjects in the New Testament with which every follower of Christ should be thoroughly acquainted, and they are its two most prominent themes: the life of Christ on earth, and the growth of the early church. In the life of Christ he should know the order of the leading events; he should grasp its principles, and should enter into its spirit. Only as we apprehend Christ can we comprehend the truths taught and inspired by Christ.

But our work as New Testament students must not end with the story of Christ's ascension from earth. Jesus left behind him a little church, of only one hundred and twenty members, which in seventy years overswept all the lands of the greatest empire then on the earth, and which now covers nearly all the world. Of that church we are members, inheritors of its traditions, its doctrines, and—best of all—its spirit. It should be our delight to trace the steps of its early progress, to see how its plans grew with the advancing years, and how an obscure company of Jewish disciples became a church of world-wide reach.

To enable a student to obtain this knowledge this book has been prepared. The earlier studies on the life of Christ have been published as Studies in the Four Gospels, but have been carefully revised and, in the author's judgment, improved. The studies on the early church are the outgrowth of work begun many years ago, frequently revised, taught to classes many times, and carefully restudied in the light of the most recent researches in the domain of early church history.

These chapters are, as their titles indicate, *studies*; designed, not for reading, but for study. This book does not undertake to be a life of Christ, and a history of the early church, to be read. It simply extends a helping hand, and holds out to the student a clue by means of which he can form his own life of Christ and prepare for himself a history of the early church. Wherever a fact can be learned by searching out a Scripture reference the fact is not stated, but the reference is given. Every text referred to should be searched out, as these texts contain the essential facts of this book. Whoever would use these studies rightly must pursue them with the Bible close at hand, and must consult his Bible more frequently than this text-book.

There are a million and a half Sunday school teachers who should be acquainted with the story of Christ and his church: and there are several millions of young people in our Sunday schools who may be teachers before many years and need the same knowledge. This book has been prepared in the hope that these teachers and young people may find it a help to know Him who is the head of the church; and to understand the church, which is the pillar and ground of truth.

Jesse L. Hurlbut.
January 3, 1906.

HINTS TO STUDENTS

Those who desire merely to *read* this book, or to look it over, will not find it interesting. Those who already know how to study will not need these hints, and can use the book in their own way. But there are many who desire to study these subjects carefully and yet do not know precisely how to do the work. For these students, earnest but untrained, these hints are given.

1. These studies should be pursued with the Bible close at hand, so that every Scripture reference may be at once searched out and read.

2. Begin each lesson by a general view; reading it through carefully, and memorizing the leading divisions of the outline, which are indicated by the Roman numerals I, II, III, etc. This will give the general plan of the lesson.

3. Now take up Part I of the lesson in detail; notice and memorize its subdivisions, indicated by 1, 2, 3, etc., and search out all the Scripture references cited in it. If practicable, write out on a sheet of paper the reference (not the language of the text in full), and what each reference shows. Thus with references in the Second Study, page 19, Section I, **Origin**, 1. **Semitic.** (Gen. 12. 1-3) God's call and promise to Abram. (Gen. 17. 1-8) The call repeated; name changed to Abraham. (James 2. 23) The Friend of God. (Gen. 18. 19: "He will command his children," etc.)

In this manner write out all the facts ascertained from all the references in the section.

4. It would be a good plan to write out in full, as a connected statement, all the facts in the section.

5. In like manner study out and write out all the facts obtained by a study of the lesson and the text cited in it. This will greatly aid the memory in holding fast to the information gained.

6. Having done this, look at the blackboard outline at the end of the study and see if you can read the outline of the lesson by the aid of the catch-words and indications which it affords. Study the lesson until you can read it with the blackboard outline, and then recall it without the outline.

7. Now take up the questions for review. Read them over, one by one, and see if you can answer them. To many of them the answer is not given

in the text-book, but it will be found in the Scripture references when searched out. Do not cease your study until every question can be answered from memory.

8. Frequently review the lessons already learned. Before beginning the third study review the first and second; before the fourth, review the first, second and third; and at the completion of the course review them all. The knowledge gained by this thorough study will more than compensate for the time and trouble which it requires.

HINTS TO TEACHERS

Classes may be organized on various plans and out of varied materials for the study of these lessons.

1. A teachers' class, composed of teachers and also of senior scholars in the Sunday school, may be formed to study the life of Christ, which is one of the most important subjects in the Bible. This may meet on an evening, or an afternoon, and devote all the session to the study of the lesson and to discussions upon it.

2. In many places a teachers' meeting is held for the study of the International Lesson as a preparation for the Sunday school class. A part of the time might be taken at this meeting for the study of these subjects. In that case it would be well to follow the division into lessons, as given on pages 11, 12.

3. A normal class may be organized among the brightest scholars in the Sunday school, who should be trained to become teachers. This normal class may meet on an afternoon, or an evening, or may take the lesson period in the Sunday school session.

4. These studies may be pursued by the young people's society of the church, or by a class formed under its auspices, meeting at such time and place as shall be found most convenient.

There are two methods in which these lessons may be taught: One is the *lecture method*, by which the instructor gives the lesson to the class in the form of a lecture, placing the outline upon the blackboard as he proceeds, calling upon the students to read the texts cited, and frequently reviewing the outline in a concert drill. By this method the students may or may not have the books, as they and the instructor prefer. While it is not necessary to supply the class with the text-book, it will be a good plan to do so. Some lecturers prefer to have the books closed while the lecture is being given; but others desire to have the students use the outline in the book as a syllabus, enabling them to follow the subject more closely.

The other method, simpler and easier, is to let the student have a copy of the book, to expect the lesson to be prepared by the class, and to have it recited, either individually or in concert. Let each student gain all the information that he can upon the subjects of the lesson; let each bring his knowledge to the possession of all; let all talk freely, and all will be the gainers.

It would be a good plan to have papers read from time to time upon the subjects suggested by the course and parallel with it.

Some teachers and classes may regard the contents of this book as too extensive and may prefer a shorter course. The aim of the author has been to include in the course only those subjects that are essential to an understanding of the New Testament, and the entire series of lessons is recommended; but if a shorter course be deemed absolutely necessary, two plans are suggested:

1. There are three subjects which under necessity might be omitted: Second Study, The People of Palestine; Third Study, General View of the Life of Christ; Twelfth Study, The Synagogue. This will leave fifteen studies, or twenty-two lessons.

2. Another plan might be undertaken: to take up as a course the studies on the life of Christ, or even omitting, as above, the second and third studies, making eight; and to leave the eight studies in the early church— a most interesting and valuable subject—to a later period.

THE COURSE DIVIDED INTO LESSONS

For the convenience of teachers and classes, the eighteen studies of this course are divided into twenty-five lessons, as follows:

Lesson 1. The Land of Palestine. First Study.
" 2. The People of Palestine. Second Study.
" 3. The Life of Christ—General View. Third Study.
" 4. The Thirty Years of Preparation. Fourth Study.
" 5. The Year of Obscurity. Fifth Study.
" 6. The Year of Popularity. Sixth Study. Part One.
" 7. The Year of Popularity. Sixth Study. Part Two.
" 8. The Year of Opposition. Seventh Study. Part One.
" 9. The Year of Opposition. Seventh Study. Part Two.
" 1   The Week of the Passion. Eighth Study.

" 10.
" 11. The Day of the Crucifixion. Ninth Study.
" 12. The Forty Days of Resurrection. Tenth Study.
" 13. The New Testament World. Eleventh Study.
" 14. The Synagogue. Twelfth Study.
" 15. The Church in Judea. Thirteenth Study. Part One.
" 16. The Church in Judea. Thirteenth Study. Part Two.
" 17. The Church in Transition. Fourteenth Study.
" 18. The Church Twenty Years after the Ascension. Fifteenth Study.
" 19. The Preparation of Paul for his Work. Sixteenth Study. Part One.
" 20. The Preparation of Paul for his Work. Sixteenth Study. Part Two.
" 21. The Church among the Gentiles. Seventeenth Study. Part One.
" 22. The Church among the Gentiles. Seventeenth Study. Part Two.
" 23. The Church among the Gentiles. Seventeenth Study. Part Three
" 24. The End of the Age. Eighteenth Study. Part One.
" 25. The End of the Age. Eighteenth Study. Part Two.

FIRST STUDY
The Land of Palestine

In the historical study of the New Testament the two principal subjects are, the life of Jesus Christ on earth and, after the Ascension, the growth of the Christian church.

The life of Christ was passed entirely in Palestine; and we therefore begin our studies with a view of that land as it was in our Saviour's day.

I. **It was an oriental land.** In all ages the boundaries of Palestine have been about the same, though the dominion of its rulers has varied according to their power. Palestine Proper, originally the land of Canaan, and later the land of Israel, or the Twelve Tribes, is located near the south-eastern corner of the Mediterranean Sea; having Syria and Phœnicia on the north, the great Syrian Desert on the east, the Sinaitic wilderness on the south, and the Mediterranean on the west. Located just outside the tropics, near the point of contact between Asia and Africa, it belongs to the Oriental or Eastern world.

II. **It was a small land.** The greatest lands have not always been the largest. Greece, no larger than half a dozen counties in America, is greater in history than vast China; and the single city of Rome won and held the empire of the Mediterranean lands. Territorially the whole extent of Palestine was about that of Massachusetts and Connecticut united, or that of Switzerland, in Europe—about 12,500 square miles. Its sea-coast, from Tyre to Gaza, is 140 miles long; its Jordan line, from Mount Hermon to the foot of the Dead Sea, is 156 miles.

III. **It was a land of varied natural features.** There is a regularity in the natural conformation of Palestine which every traveler notices. The country lies in five parallel sections.

1. Approaching from the Mediterranean one meets first a **sea-coast plain** two or three miles wide at the north, but widening, as it goes southward, to nearly twenty miles at Gaza.

2. Crossing this we approach the **Shephelah**, *or foot-hills*; a terrace of low hills, from 300 to 500 feet high.

3. Ascending these we reach **the mountain region**, a range of mountains broken by ravines in all directions, and varying from 2,500 to 3,000 feet high. This region was the home of the Israelites in all their history. They were always a mountain people and never occupied the lower plains in any great degree. In all the Bible times the plains and valleys were mainly foreign and heathen in their population, while the mountains were Israelite in the Old Testament and Jewish in the New.

4. Crossing the mountains we descend to the **Jordan valley**, lower than the sea level and from five to twenty miles wide. Through this runs the

river Jordan, passing through two lakes—Lake Merom and the Sea of Galilee—and emptying into the Dead Sea.

5. Beyond the valley rises the **eastern table-land**, with higher mountains, but more level summits, and broken by fewer valleys. The mountains gradually decline to the great Syrian Desert on the east.

IV. **It was a Land of Five Provinces.** In the time of Christ there were five political divisions in Palestine; three on the west side of Jordan and two on the east.

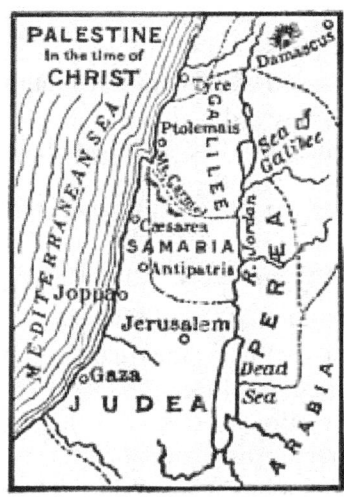

1. On the north, west of the Jordan, was the province of **Galilee**, situated between the river Jordan, the Sea of Galilee, the land of Phœnicia and Mount Carmel. It was inhabited by a brave, simple-hearted people, mainly Jews, but with many Gentiles among them. Hence its name (Isa. 9. 1, 2; Matt. 4. 15, 16); and the contempt in which it was held at Jerusalem. (John 7. 41, 52.) It was the home of Jesus during most of his life and ministry.

2. The central region was **Samaria**. See its location. (John 4. 3, 4.) It was, strictly speaking, not a province but a district around the cities of Shechem and Samaria, not extending either to the sea or river, and of uncertain limits, inhabited by a composite people, partly Israelite, partly heathen, in their origin. Note the claim of its people (John 4. 12) and their expectation. (John 4. 25.) Observe how they were regarded by the Jews. (John 4. 9; 8. 48.) Notice that Christ paid no regard to this caste prejudice. (John 4. 10.)

3. The southernmost province of Palestine was **Judea**. As the largest, and the special home of the Jewish people, it often gave its name to the whole land, as in Mark 1. 5; Luke 7. 17; Acts 10. 37. Generally,

however, it is distinguished as the name of the province, as in Luke 2. 4; Matt. 2. 22; John 4. 3. Jesus made several visits to this district, especially to its city, but only for limited periods, as its people were more bigoted than the Galileans and bitterly opposed to him.

4. On the east of the Jordan and the Dead Sea was the province of **Peræa**, a word meaning "beyond." It is not mentioned by that name in the New Testament. Notice what it is called in Matt. 19. 1; Mark 10. 1. We read of a visit paid by Jesus to this region near the close of his ministry.

5. North of the river Hieromax, and east of the Sea of Galilee, was a fifth province, the ancient land of **Bashan**, "woodland," but known in the gospels as "Philip's tetrarchy." Notice how it is specified in Luke 3. 1. Another name for a part of this territory is given in Matt. 4. 25; Mark 5. 20; 7. 31. Its inhabitants were mostly Gentiles or heathen. Twice this country enjoyed brief visits from Jesus, each marked by a miracle (Mark 5. 1-20; 7. 31-37).

V. **It was a Populous Land.** We can only note the places referred to in the gospel history, and we arrange them according to the provinces.

1. In Galilee we note: 1.) **Nazareth**, due west of the southern end of the Sea of Galilee, the early home of Jesus (Matt. 2. 23; Luke 2. 51). 2.) **Nain**, south of Nazareth, where he wrought a miracle (Luke 7. 11). 3.) **Cana**, north of Nazareth, where the first miracle was wrought (John 2. 1). 4.) **Capernaum**, on the Sea of Galilee, the home of Jesus during most of his ministry, and the scene of many miracles (Luke 4. 31; Mark 2. 1).

2. In Samaria we note two places: 1.) **Shechem**, which may be the place referred to in John 4. 5, though late authorities regard it as the name of a hamlet, now called Iskar, near by. 2.) **Samaria**, a few miles north-west of Shechem, the early capital of the province, and the first place where the Gospel was preached to other than the Jews (Acts 8. 5).

3. In the province of Judea we notice: 1.) **Jerusalem**, "the holy city" (Matt. 4. 5), and the place where Jesus was crucified (Matt. 16. 21). 2.) **Bethany**, two miles east of Jerusalem (John 11. 18), where Jesus was entertained by Mary and Martha (John 11. 1). Note two great events near this place (John 11. 43; Luke 24. 50, 51). 3.) **Bethlehem**, six miles south of Jerusalem. The great event in its history (Matt. 2. 1.) Its ancient honor (Luke 2. 4.) 4.) **Hebron**, the ancient capital of Judah, a priestly city, and the probable birthplace of John the Baptist (Luke 1. 39, 40.) 5.) **Jericho**, eighteen miles from Jerusalem, in the Jordan valley, visited by Jesus near the end of his ministry (Luke 19. 1). 6.) **Ephraim**, a village fourteen miles north of Jerusalem, the hiding place of Jesus for a brief period (John 11. 54).

4. In the province of Peræa but one place is identified as connected with the life of Christ: **Bethabara** (Revised version, "Bethany beyond the Jordan") the place of the baptism and of the first disciples; thirteen miles south of the Sea of Galilee.

5. In Philip's tetrarchy, east of the Sea of Galilee, we note three places: 1.) **Cæsarea Philippi**, at the foot of the Mount Hermon (Mark 8. 27; 9. 2). 2.) **Bethsaida**, at the head of the Sea of Galilee, east of the Jordan (Luke 9. 10-13). 3.) **Gergesa** or **Gerasa**, a little place on the eastern shore of the Sea of Galilee (Matt. 8. 28).

VI. **It was a Subject Land.** Half a century before the birth of Christ the Jews became subject to Rome, and thenceforward various changes took place in the form of government:

1. The whole land, with some surrounding provinces, was a **kingdom** under Herod the Great (Matt. 2. 1), but tributary to the emperor at Rome from 37 B. C. to 4 B. C., the year of Christ's birth.

2. On Herod's death it was divided into three **tetrarchies**, "fourth-part rules." Archelaus became tetrarch of Judea and Samaria (Matt. 2. 22); Herod Antipas, tetrarch of Galilee and Peræa (Matt. 14. 1; Luke 23. 6, 7); Herod Philip, tetrarch of the Bashan district (Luke 3. 1). A fourth tetrarchy, outside of Palestine, on the north, was held by Lysanias (Luke 3. 1).

3. About the year 7 A. D., when Jesus was eleven years old, Archelaus was deposed by the Roman emperor and his dominion made a province under a Roman procurator, the other two tetrarchies remaining undisturbed. This was the form of government during the ministry of Jesus. Judea and Samaria constituting one Roman province under Pontius Pilate; Galilee and Peræa, Herod's tetrarchy, and Bashan, Philip's tetrarchy.

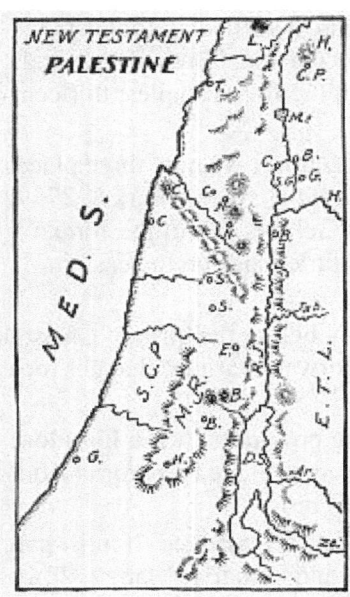

4. In the year 37 the Roman emperor made Herod Agrippa I. king first over Judea, and then, in 41, over all the dominions of his grandfather, so that Palestine became a kingdom again. He is mentioned in Acts 12. 1.

5. On Agrippa's death, in A. D. 44, a new division took place. Agrippa II., son of Agrippa I., became ruler of Chalcis and Bashan. He is called, but by courtesy only, "King Agrippa," in Acts 25. 13; 26. 1, 2. The rest of Palestine, consisting of Judea, Samaria, and Peræa, became again a procuratorship under direct Roman rule. See Acts 23. 24; 24. 27.

6. On the rebellion of the Jews, A. D. 66, the government was again changed. Palestine became a part of Syria, under Vespasian, the legate. This was the end of Jewish history as a separate nationality.

Suggestions for Study and Teaching

1. Study carefully a good map of Palestine and learn from it the boundaries and location of the land. Memorize the dimensions and distances given in the outline.

2. Draw a map showing the five natural divisions in Par. III., and learn their names.

3. Indicate on your own map the five provinces, comparing the best maps at hand to find their boundary lines.

4. Locate on your own map all the places named in Par. V., and be able to name an event connected with each, studying the references for this purpose.

5. Be sure to examine all the references, and state what fact each reference shows concerning a locality.

6. Draw in succession five sketch maps, each to represent the political government of a period. Write across each province the name of a ruler. Map No. 1 will represent it at the birth of Christ. No. 2, during the childhood of Christ. Map No. 3, during his ministry. No. 4, about A. D. 41. No. 5, from 42 to 66 A. D. Look out all the references given in Par. VI.

Blackboard Outline

I. **Orien. L. Bound.** N. S. P. E. S. D. S. S. W. W. M. S.

II. **Sm. L.** S. M. 12,500. S. C. 140. J. L. 156.

III. **Var. Nat. Fea.** S. C. P. Sh. M. R. J. V. E. T. L.

IV. **Fiv. Prov.** Gal. Sam. Jud. Per. Bash.

V. **Pop. L.** Gal. N. N. C. C. Sam. Sh. Sa. Jud. J. B. B. H. J. E. Per. B. Ph. Tet. C. P. B. G.

V. **Sub. L.** 1. Km. 2. Tetr. 3. Prov. 4. Kgm. 5. "Kg. Ag." Rom. Proc. 6. I. Part of Syr.

Questions for Review

Why do we need to study the land of Palestine? What were the boundaries of Palestine? Where is it located? Name some small countries which have been prominent in history. What is the size of Palestine? How long is the coast-line? The Jordan line? What are the five natural divisions of the land? Name and bound each of the political divisions. In which of these provinces was Jesus born? In which did he pass most of his life? In which was he crucified? Name four places in Galilee, and an event connected with each? Two places in Samaria, and their events. Six places in Judea and their events. One place in Peræa and three in Philip's tetrarchy, with their events. State the six successive forms of government and their rulers in Palestine during the New Testament period.

SECOND STUDY
The People of Palestine

In all the ancient world there was but one people among whom Christ could have come with his revelation, and through whom his message could have been given to mankind. That people was **the Jews**, in certain respects the most remarkable of all the races.

I. We notice their **origin**, which shows a series of selections extending through many centuries and a training for their peculiar mission.

1. Of the three great families of earth, they sprang from the **Semitic**, which has been the mother of all the great religions of the world; a thoughtful, meditative race, rather than active and aggressive.

2. From this race **Abraham** was called, more than twenty centuries before Christ, to be the father of a great nation (Gen. 12. 1-3; 17. 1-8). He was distinguished for his worship of the one God, for his faith, and for his nobility of character. Notice his title in Jas. 2. 23; a name by which he is still known in the East, *el Khalil*, "the Friend." His influence upon his family (Gen. 18. 19).

3. Of the families descended from Abraham that of **Isaac** was chosen (Gen. 21. 12; Rom. 9. 7). All the other races of Abrahamic origin yielded to the idolatrous influences around them and lost the knowledge of God.

4. Of the two sons of Isaac one married among the Canaanites, and, as a result, his descendants became idolaters (Gen. 26. 34, 35; 36. 2). The other chose the inheritance of the covenant (Gen. 28. 20-22). His name was changed (Gen. 32. 28; 35. 10). His descendants, the **Israelites**, trained up in the true faith, became the people of God. Each of his twelve sons was the ancestor of a tribe (Exod. 1. 1-7). They continued one people for a thousand years, though part of the time divided into two kingdoms.

5. In the year 721 B. C. ten of the twelve tribes were carried into Assyrian captivity (2 Kings 17. 18-20). Having lost their religion, the only bond of unity, they mingled with the idolatrous world and ceased to be a separate people. The **tribe of Judah** was left, Benjamin being incorporated with it. Henceforth they were called "the Jews," a name found first in 2 Kings 18. 26.

6. But through all the history of Judah, as well as of Israel, there had been two distinct elements in the people: the worshipers of God and of idols; the religious and the worldly. In order to separate these elements, to cut off the evil and to discipline the good, came the Babylonian captivity, B. C. 587. Through this the idolatrous element was either destroyed or assimilated with the heathen world. At the release from captivity, B. C. 536, all the Jews were of God-fearing, Scripture-loving element. This was **the Remnant**, the "holy seed," the true Israel (Isa. 6. 8-13).

Thus, out of all the world, was gradually chosen and prepared a people among whom the Lord should come.

II. Notice **their traits** as a race, for which they were chosen, and which were intensified by their training:

1. They were a **religious** people; monotheistic; worshiping the one invisible God, hating idolatry. See the command (Exod. 20. 3-6). The exhortation of Joshua (Josh. 24. 14). This is the great glory of Israel alone among the ancient nations.

2. They were an **exclusive** people; strongly attached to each other, and seeking no affiliation with other races. Note this trait in Abraham (Gen. 24. 2-4). Also in Isaac (Gen. 28. 1, 2). See Balaam's prophecy (Num. 23. 9). To this day the Jews dwell apart; in most European cities there is a "Jewish quarter."

3. They were a **conservative** people; attached to their own customs, opposed to all changes, clinging to their worship despite persecution.

4. They were an **aspiring** people. From their earliest history the Jews cherished the expectation of being a great and conquering nation. From their own prophecies they obtained the hope and belief that a great king should arise among them to rule the world. See the promises in Gen. 49. 10. The prophecy in Isa. 32. 1, 2. His title in Dan. 9. 25. The word "Messiah" in Hebrew is "Christos" in Greek, and "Anointed" in English. This messianic hope was the central thought of all Judaism.

5. They were a **moral** people. Their Scripture set up a standard of character immeasurably superior to that in other ancient lands. Among the Jews womanhood was honored, drunkenness was rare, honesty was the rule, and crime was far less frequent than elsewhere.

These were the traits that made the Jews the people of God and fitted them to accomplish the divine purpose.

III. What was that purpose? Every race has its mission in the world. The Greeks were set to exalt the intellect; the Romans, to establish the reign of law. We notice the **mission of the Jewish people**:

1. **To perpetuate the knowledge of God.** In the general wickedness of the world and the spread of idolatry there was danger lest the true religion be utterly lost. Therefore God chose out one nation—the one having the traits best fitting it for his purpose—and set it apart to guard the holy fire of divine truth until the rest of the world should be ready to receive it.

2. **To receive training for higher revelation.** The higher revelations of God can come only to a people whose religious faculties have been trained to receive them. Judaism was God's school where a chosen race was educated. They received the Scriptures, the prophets, the ritual of

worship, and, above all, the discipline of trial, fitting them to become "a nation of priests." See Paul's enumeration of their privileges in Rom. 9. 4, 5.

3. **To proclaim the Gospel to the world.** When, in the fullness of time, Israel was trained up to knowledge and the outer world prepared to receive the truth, Christ came as the consummation of Judaism. Then a new mission opened before the Jews—that of proclaiming Christ to the world. The little company of disciples were the seed that should replenish the whole earth. See the command. (Matt. 28. 19, 20.)

IV. We notice now the **Jews in the time of Christ**.

1. They were divided into two great **branches**: the **Jews of Palestine** and the **Jews of the Dispersion**. The former were descendants of those who had settled in Palestine after the decree of Cyrus, B. C. 536 (Ezra 1. 1-3); the latter those who remained in the lands of their adoption, were found all over the ancient world, and were far more numerous. See references to them in John 7. 35; James 1. 1; 1 Pet. 1. 1. We note that these "Jews of the Dispersion" were not descendants of the Ten Tribes, except in a few instances, but were *Jews*—that is, descendants of Judah.

2. Noticing now the Palestinian Jews, for with these the life of Christ was mainly connected, we find them divided into two **sects**, or schools of thought: the **Pharisees** and the **Sadducees**. These two parties arose about 168 B. C., in the time of the Maccabæan uprising. Let us look at them in contrast.

1.) Their *names* express their traits. *Pharisee* means "separatist," "one who is apart." *Sadducee* means "just," or "righteous," but rather with our idea of the world "moralist."

2.) Their *aims*. The Pharisee aimed to keep the Mosaic law absolutely, particularly with regard to ceremonial requirements; to do more than obey it, by setting around it a hedge of traditional interpretations going beyond its letter in strictness. The Sadducee professed to keep the law, ignoring tradition, but gave it a lax and easy interpretation which often ignored its requirements.

3.) Their *spirit*. The Pharisee was the radical and zealot, showing an intense, intolerant Judaism. The Sadducee was the liberal easy-going man of the world, taking the world as he found it.

4.) Their *beliefs*. The Pharisee believed in a spiritual world, heaven, hell, angels, the hereafter, the judgment. The Sadducee could not find clear statements of these doctrines in the Old Testament, and denied them. See Matt. 22. 23; Acts 23. 8.

5.) Their *influence*. The Pharisees were strong in the synagogues, where the scribes gave their interpretations, and hence were powerful among the people as leaders in religion. The Sadducees were the smaller body, but influential from their wealth and their social position, for the high priests and all the priestly order belonged to them, and they were the office-holding class, the court party. (Acts 4. 1, 2; 5. 17.)

6.) Their *evils*. The evil of the Pharisees was their tendency to make religion mere hypocritical formality, so often rebuked by Christ. See Matt. 23. 2-7. The evil of the Sadducees was their utter lack of moral conviction, from worldliness and self-interest. See their motive for putting Christ to death (John 11. 47-50).

3. Thus far we have noticed only Jews, but there were also in Palestine many **Gentiles**, which was the name the Jews gave to all foreigners or people of race other than themselves. These were of three classes, called respectively: 1.) **Sinners**—That is, those who made no attempt to observe Jewish usages. See Gal. 2. 15. The same name was given to the Jews who did not undertake to keep the ceremonial law, without reference to their moral character (Matt. 9. 10, 11). 2.) **The Devout.** Those who believed in the Scriptures and worshiped God, but who had not been received into the Jewish Church by circumcision. Such was Cornelius (Acts 10. 1, 2). 3.) **Proselytes**—Such as renounced Gentilism, received circumcision, and obeyed the Jewish law (Acts 6. 5; Matt. 23. 15).

V. **The Language of Palestine.**

1. Originally **Hebrew**; still read, in Christ's time, in the synagogue but not well understood and requiring an interpreter.

2. Mostly **Aramaic**, or **Syro-Chaldaic**—that is, Chaldaic with Syrian admixture; the common dialect of the people, and undoubtedly spoken by Christ. See instances in Mark 7. 34; 15. 34. This is the language referred to in John 19. 20, 21, and Acts 22. 2, as "Hebrew."

3. The language of polite literature in all countries was **Greek**; strongly opposed by the Pharisees, but employed by the Jews of the Dispersion, and used in the courts of Herod and Pilate (Acts 21. 37).

4. The official language was **Latin**, that of the Roman Government, but not used by the Jews, and not generally understood by them.

Blackboard Outline

I. **Origin.**—1. Sem. 2. Abr. 3. Isa. 4. Isr. (12 t.) 5. Jud (Jews). 6. "Remn."

II **Traits.**—1. Rel. 2. Exc. 3. Cons. 4. Asp. "Mess." 5. Mor.

III. **Mission.**—1. Per. kno. G. 2. Rec. tra. hi. rev. 3. Pro. Gos. wo.

IV. **Jews Ti. Chr.**—1. Bran. Pal. Dis. 2. Sec. Phar. Sadd. 1.) Nam. 2.) Aim. 3.) Spir. 4.) Bel. 5.) Inf. 6.) Evils. 3. Gen. 1.) Sin. 2.) "Dev." 3.) Pro.

V. **Lang.**—1. Heb. 2. Ara. (Syr.-Chal.). 3. Gre. 4. Lat.

Questions for Review

To what people did Jesus Christ belong? From what great family of races did that people spring? What were the traits of this race? Who was the ancestor of the Jews, and what were his traits of character? How were the Jews gradually selected from among the descendants of Abraham? To which of the twelve tribes did most of the Jews belong? What was "the remnant" in Old Testament history? Name five traits of the Jews as a people. What was the mission of the Jewish people? What were the two great branches of the Jews in the time of Christ? What were their two sects? What were the differences between these sects? Who were the Gentiles? Into what three classes were they divided? What four languages were found among the Jews in the time of Christ?

THIRD STUDY

The Life of Christ

The central figure in all the Bible is Jesus Christ. Note his importance in the Old Testament (John 5. 39; Luke 24. 27; Acts 10. 43). Note his prominence in all true gospel teaching (1 Cor. 2. 2). Note his relation to every man (John 1. 9.) (Rev. Ver.) We have, then, an interest in Jesus Christ deeper than in any other man who ever lived.

I. Let us notice some **General Aspects of his Life**.

1. It was a **short** life. This man, who has influenced the world more than any other, lived less than thirty-five years. His age at the beginning of his ministry we learn from Luke 3. 23; and the duration of his ministry was not more than three years and a half at the longest.

2. It was a life **passed wholly in Palestine**. Only once do we read of his journeying near any other country, and it is not probable that he went

beyond its borders (Mark 7. 24). The only times of direct contact with Gentiles are mentioned (Mark 7. 25, 26; John 12. 20-22). He never enjoyed the benefits of foreign travel, of communion with learned men in the great cities, of studies at the universities of Athens or Alexandria. All his knowledge came from within.

3. It was a life **among the common people**. He lived in a despised province (John 7 41, 52). He came from a despised town (John 1. 46). He was a working mechanic (Mark 6. 3). He received only a common education (John 7. 15). His manner of life during his ministry (Matt. 8. 20). Yet out of these lowly surroundings grew up the one exalted character, the one perfect life, in all human history.

4. It was an **active** life. The first thirty years may have been spent in quiet preparation, but the three years of his ministry were very busy. See pictures in Mark 1. 36-38; 2. 1-4; 6. 31-34. Notice the hyperbole in John 21. 25, which is not to be taken literally. But if the whole life of Jesus were related with the minuteness of the day between the sunset of the Last Supper and that of the burial the narration would require one hundred and eighty-five books as large as the Bible.

II. Let us arrange the events of Christ's life in chronological order, grouping them into **Seven Periods**.

1. The first period is that of **The Thirty Years of Preparation**, of which we notice the following facts:

1.) It begins with his Birth (Luke 2. 7), and ends with his Temptation (Matt. 4. 1).

2.) It is related mainly by Luke (Luke 1-4) with some facts in Matthew (Matt. 1. 2; 4. 1-11), and a brief mention of its closing events in Mark (Mark 1. 9-13).

3.) It was passed mainly in Galilee, though with isolated events in Judea, in Egypt (Matt. 2. 14, 15), and in Peræa. See John 1. 28.

4.) It was the longest of all the periods, embracing nine-tenths of his life; yet it is the one having the fewest incidents recorded; and of eighteen years in it absolutely no events are known.

2. Next is **The Year of Obscurity**. In this and the two succeeding periods the year is not a precise epoch, and may have been a little less or a little more.

1.) It begins with the first followers (John 1. 35-37), and ends with the return to Galilee (John 4. 43, 44).

2.) It is related only by John, who, of all the gospel writers, records the visit of Jesus to Judea and Jerusalem.

3.) It was passed principally in Judea, though with visits to Galilee, and on the way a visit to Samaria.

4.) It is justly called a "year of obscurity," for we know but little concerning either its aims, its events, or its results. It was accompanied with miracles (John 3. 2; 4. 45). It attracted attention (John 3. 26; 4. 1). Yet at its close we find that the followers of Jesus were few, and he went to Galilee to begin his ministry anew.

3. **The Year of Popularity**, in marked contrast with the preceding period.

1.) It begins with the Rejection at Nazareth (Luke 4. 14-30), and ends with the Discourse on the Bread of Life (John 6. 25-71), a day or two after the miracle of Feeding the Five Thousand.

2.) It is related by Matthew, Mark, and Luke, with some additional incidents by John.

3.) The scene of the Saviour's ministry was in Galilee, which he traversed extensively during this year. One visit to Jerusalem is related by John (John 5. 1, 2).

4.) It was a year of great activity, spent in incessant journeys, preaching, and works of mercy, and the most popular period of the Saviour's life, when the crowds were greatest and the people seemed ready to accept Jesus as the Messiah of Israel. Yet at its close, as before, he was left alone with his twelve disciples (John 6. 66-68).

4. Another period we find in **The Year of Opposition**, again contrasted with the year before it.

1.) It begins with the Retirement to Phœnicia (Mark 7. 24) and ends with the Anointing by Mary (John 12. 1-3).

2.) It is recorded in all the gospels in almost equal measure, Luke giving the most complete account of the ministry in Peræa, and John, as usual, relating the visit to Judea.

3.) This period is peculiar in the fact that in it Jesus visited all the five provinces of Palestine. We find him in Decapolis (which was a part of the Bashan district) (Mark 7. 31); passing through Galilee (Mark 9. 30); also through Samaria (Luke 9. 51, 52); in Peræa (Mark 10. 1), and in Judea (John 11. 7).

4.) This part of the Saviour's life has been variously characterized as "a ministry of sorrow and humiliation," "a year of instruction," and "a period of retirement." All are correct, for during this, the last year of his life, Jesus sought to be alone with his disciples, and in order to escape the crowds visited places where he was unknown. He aimed to instruct his disciples in the deeper truths of the gospel, to prepare their minds for his approaching death and for their mission as apostles (Matt. 16. 21).

5. We now approach the close of Christ's life on earth, and the narration is more detailed as the cross comes nearer to view. Our next period is **The Week of the Passion**.

1.) Beginning with the Triumphal Entry on the Sunday before the Passover (John 21. 12, 13), it ends with the Agony in the Garden about midnight on Thursday (Matt. 26. 36); thus embracing strictly but five days.

2.) It is related in all the gospels, John alone adding the teaching given at the Last Supper (John 13-17).

3.) All the events of this period took place in or near Jerusalem.

4.) This was the last call of Christ to the Jews of Jerusalem, and his final rebuke for their rejection of his ministry.

6. **The Day of the Crucifixion.** The most important day in all earth's history was that when Jesus died upon the cross. It is also the day whose events are narrated more fully than any other in the Bible annals. Therefore we study it apart from the rest of the week as a separate period.

1.) It begins with the Arrest (Matt. 26. 47), soon after midnight, Friday A. M., the day of the Passover, and ends at about sunset of the same day with the Burial (Matt. 27. 59, 60).

2.) Each gospel adds its portion to the account, that of John, an eye-witness of all the events, being the most complete.

3.) The events took place in Jerusalem; but few, if any, of the localities are known with certainty.

4.) In the scenes of this day we see Jesus as the suffering Saviour, bearing the sins of the world.

7. Last of all come **The Forty Days of Resurrection**.

1.) From the Resurrection, early on the first Easter Sunday (Matt. 28. 1-8), to the Ascension, forty days afterward (Acts 1. 1-3).

2.) All the gospels give accounts of the appearances of the risen Saviour, but Luke alone tells the story of his Ascension (Luke 24. 50, 51; Acts 1. 9-11).

3.) The manifestations of Christ after his Resurrection took place in and near Jerusalem, near the village of Emmaus (Luke 24. 13), and in Galilee (Matt. 28. 16; John 21. 1).

4.) During this period the visible revelation of Christ was not constant, but occasional; to his disciples only, never to his enemies; and of a spiritual body, which was freed from the restraints of the flesh (Mark 16. 12; Luke 24. 31; John 20. 19).

Blackboard Outline

I. **Gen. Asp.** 1. Sh. 2. In Pal. 3 Am. com. peo. 4. Ac.

II. **Sev. Per.**

1. **Th. Ye. Prep.** 1) Bir-Temp. 2) Lu. Mat. Mar. 3) Gal. 4) Long. few inc.

2. **Ye. Obs.** 1) Fir. Foll.-Re. Gal. 2) Jno. 3) Jud. 4) Obs.

3. **Ye. Pop.** 1) Re. Naz-Dis. B. L. 2) M. M. L. 3) Gal. 4) Act.

4. **Ye. Opp.** 1) Re. Ph.-An. Ma. 2) All Gos. 3) All Prov. 4) Instruc.

5. **We. Pass.** 1) Tri. En.-Ag. Gar. 2) All Gos. 3) Jer. 4) Las. Ca.

6. **Day Cru.** 1) Arr.-Bur. 2) All Gos. 3) Jer. 4) Suff. Sav.

7. **For. Da. Res.** 1) Res.-Asc. 2) All Gos. 3) Jud. Gal. 4) Spir. bod.

Questions for Review

In what respects is Jesus Christ the central figure in the Bible? How long was Christ's life on the earth? Where was it passed? Among what class of people did Jesus live? How do we know that Jesus led an active life? What is the first of the seven periods into which his life is divided? With what events does the first period begin and end? Which gospel relates the most of this period? Where was it mainly passed? How long was it? What is the second period called? What are its first and last events? By whom is it related? Where was it passed? What were its results? What is the third period called? With what events did it begin and end? By what evangelists is it related? In what province was it passed? What is the fourth period called? With what events did it begin and end? What provinces were visited during this period? What were the traits of Christ's ministry at this time? What is the fifth period called? How long was it? What in this period is related by but one evangelist? Where did its events take place? What is the sixth period called? How long was it? With what events did it begin and end? Which account is most complete? What is the seventh and last period called? What were its first and last events? Which gospel alone relates the ascension? What were the traits of Jesus during those days?

FOURTH STUDY

The Thirty Years of Preparation

From the Birth of Jesus to His Temptation.

We have before us the longest of all the divisions in the history of Jesus, embracing thirty of his thirty-three years of life, and the one concerning which we know the least.

I. Let us study the **Places** connected with this period. These we group according to locality, and not in the order of their events. Beginning in the north and traveling southward we note the following places:

1. **Nazareth, his early home**, in Galilee, due west of the southern point of the Sea of Galilee. Here Joseph and Mary lived before the birth of Jesus (Luke 2. 39); here Jesus was brought up (Luke 4. 16); and here he was living up to the time of his baptism (Mark 1. 9).

2. **Bethabara** (Rev. Ver., Bethany), **the place of his baptism**. This was in the Jordan valley, south of the Sea of Galilee. (John 1. 28).

3. **The wilderness, the place of his temptation.** (Matt. 4. 1.) This was probably the rocky desolate region of Judea, near the head of the Dead Sea.

4. **Jerusalem, the place of the Temple**; the Jewish capital, due west of the northern point of the Dead Sea. Find three visits of Jesus to the temple during this period. 1.) In his infancy (Luke 2. 22). 2.) In his youth (Luke 2. 42). 3.) In his manhood (Luke 4. 9).

5. **Bethlehem, the place of his birth.** (Matt. 2. 1). This was six miles south of Jerusalem, in Judea.

6. **Egypt, the place of his refuge.** (Matt. 2. 14). This was the land south-west of Palestine, where Jesus was taken in his infancy in order to escape from King Herod.

Let the student 1.) Draw a map showing these places. 2.) Memorize the list. 3.) With each place name its event in the life of Jesus. 4.) Find other events of Scripture history connected with these places.

II. Let us arrange in order the **Events** of this period. 1. **The annunciation of his birth.** 1.) To Mary (Luke 1. 26-38). 2.) To Joseph (Matt. 1. 20, 21). 3.) To Simeon (Luke 2. 25, 26). 4.) To the shepherds (Luke 2. 8-11).

2. **The birth at Bethlehem.** Note the purpose for which Joseph and Mary went to Bethlehem (Luke 2. 1-4). The circumstances of his birth (Luke 2. 6, 7).

3. **The welcome to the child.** 1.) On the night of his birth (Luke 2. 15). 2.) A few days later (Matt. 2. 1, 11). 3.) In the temple (Luke 2. 25-28, 36, 38).

4. **The refuge in Egypt** (Matt. 2. 13-15). This may have been for a few weeks, a few months, or for a few years.

5. **The childhood at Nazareth** (Matt. 2. 22, 23; Luke 2. 39, 40). By what route would the journey from Egypt be made?

6. **The visit to the temple.** Read the account in Luke 2. 41-52, and notice: 1.) The age of Jesus. 2.) The object of the journey. 3.) Probable route. 4.) Where he tarried and why. 5.) The objects of his interest. 6.) Traits of his character shown.

7. **The silent years.** From the age of twelve to that of thirty no events are named. His home was still at Nazareth (John 1. 45).

8. **The woodworker at Nazareth.** From the fact that Joseph is not referred to after the visit to the temple it may be presumed that he died before the ministry of Jesus began. He had been a "carpenter" (Matt. 13. 35); although the word means, more precisely, "a skilled worker in wood," and may refer to the making of almost anything except houses, which were not built of wood. Jesus followed the same trade (Mark 6. 3) and, as the oldest son, supported his widowed mother and younger brothers and sisters (Mark 6. 3).

9. **The baptism in Jordan.** Compare the four accounts (Matt. 3. 13-17; Mark 1. 9-11; Luke 3. 21, 22; John 1. 28-34); and find: 1.) The place. 2.) The age of Jesus. 3.) The baptizer. 4.) The divine manifestation.

10. **The temptation in the wilderness.** This followed immediately upon the baptism, and was a preparation for his ministry (Matt. 4. 1-11; Mark 1. 12, 13; Luke 4. 1-13). Note: 1.) The place. 2.) The personality of the tempter. 3.) The three forms of temptation. 4.) How repelled. 5.) The result.

Let the student, 1.) Memorize these nine events in their order. 2.) Read the account of each in the gospels. 3.) Recall where each took place. 4.) Notice what other persons besides Jesus are named in the period (for example, Joseph, Mary, Simeon, Anna, Herod, etc.) and each one's part in the events.

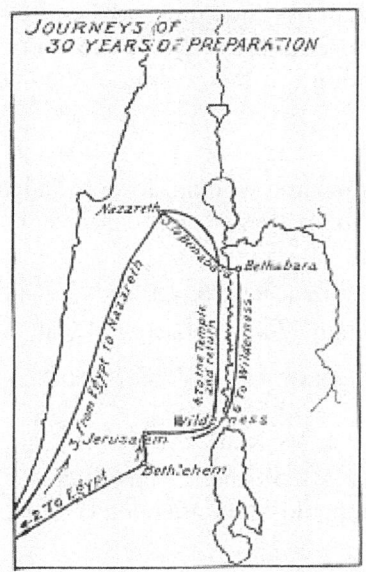

III. Draw the map of Palestine, locating upon it the live places named; and then indicate the following **Journeys** of the period: 1. From Bethlehem to Jerusalem (for the presentation in the temple) and return. 2. From Bethlehem to Egypt (flight from Herod). 3. From Egypt to Nazareth. 4. From Nazareth to Jerusalem and return (visit to temple). 5. From Nazareth to Bethabara (baptism). 6. Bethabara to the wilderness (temptation).

IV. Let us now study the **External Conditions** of Christ's life during this period.

1. **The family.** The royal line of both Joseph and Mary (Matt. 1. 1; Luke 1. 27, 32). Their obscure social condition (Matt. 13. 54, 55). In all probability they belonged to the better class of self-supporting workers: for Joseph followed a trade.

2. **The house.** Probably like those of working people in Palestine; built of clay, one story high, containing but one room with no window, but lighted through the door; whitewashed on the outside; floor of earth.

3. **The furniture.** A couch that could be rolled up (Mark 2. 12). A lamp, a lamp-stand, "the bushel" (used as seat, table, and dish (Matt. 5. 15). Hand-mill for grinding (Deut. 24. 6; Matt. 24. 41). Probably neither chair, table, nor bedstead.

4. **Education.** Jesus received only the common schooling, not a college education (John 7. 15). Contrast with the early advantages of Paul (Acts

22. 3). Every synagogue had a school taught by "the minister." See Luke 4. 20. He was not a priest, nor even a scribe, but properly the curator or sexton of the synagogue, and all the teaching was the reading of the Old Testament.

5. **Religious training.**

1.) There was the influence of a godly man and woman. Joseph, "a just man," living in fellowship with God. (Matt. 1. 19, 20). The character of Mary (Luke 1. 38; 2. 19, 51).

2.) The instruction in the Scriptures at home (Deut. 6. 7.)

3.) The daily prayers, morning and evening, always observed (Matt. 6. 5, 6).

4.) The Sabbath rest (Mark 2. 27).

5.) The worship of the synagogue (Luke 4. 16; Mark 6. 2.)

6.) The great feasts, celebrated each year at Jerusalem—Passover, Pentecost, and Tabernacles—which Joseph and Mary attended (Luke 2. 41).

Under these influences Jesus grew up to manhood.

Blackboard Outline

I. **Pla.** 1. Naz. ea. h. 2. Beth. pl. bap. 3. Wil. pl. temp. 4. Jer. pl. Tem. 5. Beth. pl. bir. 6. Eg. pl. ref.

II **Even.** 1. Ann. bir. 2. Bir. Beth. 3. Wel. ch. 4. Ref. Eg. 5. Chi. Naz. . 6. Vis. Tem. 7. Sil. ye. 8. Wo. Naz. 9. Bap. Jor. 10. Tem. wil.

III. **Jour.** 1. B. J. R. 2. B. E. 3. E. N. 4. N. J. R. 5. N. C. 6. B. W.

IV. **Ext. Con.** 1. Fam. 2. Hou. 3. Furn. 4. Edu. 5. Rel. tra.

Questions for Review

Where did the mother of Jesus live before her marriage? At what place was Jesus baptized? Where did the temptation take place? What three visits did Jesus make to Jerusalem before his ministry? To what country was Jesus taken as a refuge from Herod? Name six places connected with this period and a fact about each. Name four announcements made to different people of the coming of Jesus. For what purpose did Joseph and Mary go to Bethlehem just before the birth of Jesus? Who came to see Jesus at Bethlehem. Who gave him welcome in the temple during his infancy? How old was Jesus when he first visited the temple? What part of his life is known as "the silent years"? What trade did Jesus follow when he became a man? What took place at the baptism of Jesus? State nine events in the first thirty years of Jesus's life. State a fact in the life of Jesus with which each of the following persons was connected: Joseph, Simeon, Herod, John the Baptist, Gabriel, wise men, "the doctors of the law," shepherds. How do we know that Joseph and Mary were poor people? To what distinguished family did they belong? In what kind of a house did they probably dwell? What articles of furniture did the house contain? What education did Jesus receive? Who was the teacher of the school? What were the religious influences around the youth of Jesus? What feasts did he attend?

FIFTH STUDY

The Year of Obscurity

From the First Followers of Jesus to His Return to Galilee.

I. **Preliminary Notes** on the period.

1. **Sources of Information.** Our only account of this period is contained in **John's Gospel**. Read carefully John 1. 19 to 4. 54 for all the facts on record.

2. **Time.** The Saviour came from the temptation in the wilderness either late in February or early in March, A. D. 27, and he began his ministry in Galilee in May, A. D. 28; so that this period embraced nearly **fifteen months**. (Edersheim. According to Andrews it ended in March, and was a year in duration).

3. **Locality.** Most of this year was passed in **Judea**, though there is mention of one journey to **Galilee** soon after the beginning (John 1. 43), and of another at the close (John 4. 3).

4. **Aim.** It is probable that Jesus began his ministry in Judea, the leading province, in order to give to the leaders of the nation the **first opportunity** of accepting him as the Messiah of Israel. Not until Jerusalem and Judea had rejected him did he turn to the people of Galilee.

II. **Places.**

1. **Bethabara** (or Bethany, as in Rev. Ver.) (John 1. 28). Here occurred the meeting of Jesus with his first followers (John 1. 37).

2. **Cana**, the place of the first miracle (John 2. 1). This was in Galilee, not far from Nazareth.

3. **Capernaum**, named only as a place of a brief visit by Jesus at this time, but later more prominent in the history (John 2. 12). Situated on the north-western shore of the Sea of Galilee.

4. **Sychar**, the place of the Samaritan ministry (John 4. 5, 40). This was formerly supposed to be the well-known city of Shechem, but is now more accurately fixed at *Askar*, a small village near to Jacob's well.

5. **Jerusalem.** During this period two events took place in Jerusalem—the cleansing of the temple (John 2. 14, 15), and the conversation with Nicodemus (John 3. 1-21).

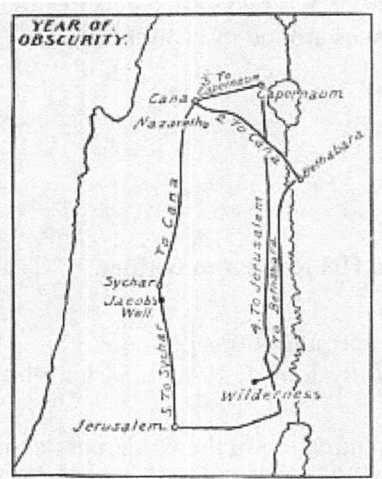

III. **Journeys.** We begin in the wilderness of the temptation. 1. From the wilderness to Bethabara. 2. From Bethabara to Cana. 3. From Cana to Capernaum. 4. From Capernaum to Jerusalem and Judea. 5. From Judea to Sychar, and thence to Cana.

IV. We place in order next the **Events** of the Saviour's life during this period.

1. **The first followers.** Read John 1. 35-51 and ascertain the names of four, with hints of two others; for one of two in ver. 40 was John, and the language in ver. 41 implies that each sought his own brother. Notice what traits of character each disciple showed. In this little company, the band out of which grew the Christian Church, we find: 1.) A man who brought people one by one to Jesus. 2.) A deep, spiritually-minded mystic. 3.) A born leader. 4.) A plain, simple-minded believer. 5.) A man of pure, spotless character. What a combination of qualities for the founding of a church!

2. **The first miracle** (John 2. 1-11). In this miracle we find an apt symbol of what Christ came to do among men. He found water, and he turned it into living, spirit-quickening wine.

3. **The visit to Capernaum** (John 2. 12). Why he went we have no means of knowing, and it is idle to speculate.

4. **The first Passover** (John 2. 13). The mention of these passovers is important, for they enable us to know how long was the ministry of Jesus, and they give us dates for its events. This was the first passover of his ministry, not of his life.

5. **Cleansing the Temple** (John 2. 14-17). This was the first public act of his ministry in which he claimed the authority of Messiah in the house of God. See the prophecy, Mal. 3. 1-3. At the close of his ministry he found that the same evils had crept again into the temple, and purged it a second time (Matt. 21. 12).

6. **Conversation with Nicodemus** (John 3. 1-21). This conversation was remarkable: 1.) From the rank and character of the man (Vers. 3, 10). 2.) From the theme (Ver. 3.) 3). From its results (John 7. 50; 19. 39).

7. **Ministry in Judea** (John 3. 22.) 1.) Its precise place is unknown. 2.) Its relation to John the Baptist (John 3. 26). 3.) Its success (John 4. 1).

8. **Ministry in Samaria** (John 4. 4-42). 1.) What led to it. (Ver. 4.) 2.) Where it took place. (Ver. 5.) 3.) How it began. (Vers. 6, 7.) 4.) Its first convert, a remarkable character, of aptness in speech, penetration, and power to influence others. (Vers. 9, 15, 20, 25, 28, 30, 39.) Compare her brightness with the dullness of Nicodemus. 5.) Its length. (Ver. 40.) 6.) Its results: (Vers. 41, 42.) This ministry is a most interesting episode in the life of Jesus.

9. **Return to Galilee** (John 4. 43). 1.) Reason for the journey (John 4. 1-3). 2.) Another reason (Mark 1. 14). 3.) Still another reason (John 4. 44, 45)—that is, he had no honor in his own country until he had obtained it in Judea.

10. **Healing the nobleman's son** (John 4. 46-54). 1.) Where Jesus was. (Ver. 46.) 2.) Who the man was. (Ver. 46)—literally, "a king's man, courtier." Is his name given in Luke 8. 30? 3.) His spirit, earnestness, persistence, faith. (Vers. 48-50.) 4.) His reward. (Vers. 51, 52.) 5.) Result of the miracle. (Ver. 53.)

Let the student, 1.) Commit this series to memory. 2.) Study the facts in relation to each by searching out the references. 3.) Recall the facts in connection with each event. 4.) Make a list of eight men and two women who were connected with these events and recall what is related of each person.

V. Let us now consider the **General Traits of the Ministry of Christ** during this period.

1. It was **preparatory**. So far as we can perceive, the plans of Christ's kingdom were not as yet revealed, and no general proclamation of it was

made. Yet he clearly revealed himself to a chosen few as the Messiah of Israel (John 1. 41, 45: 4. 25, 26).

2. **It was connected with John the Baptist.** The two streams of John's ministry and Christ's ministry run together during this preparatory ministry. John introduced Jesus (John 1. 29-36). The two worked at the same time, in the same way, and not far apart (John 3. 22-24). Both Jesus and John refused to be put into a relation of rivalry, either by their friends (John 3. 25-30) or by their enemies (John 4. 1-3).

3. It was **individual**—that is, to individuals rather than to masses of people. We read of no such multitudes as in the succeeding period, but we find six conversations of Jesus with single persons or small groups. He sought to gather a few choice disciples rather than many adherents.

4. It was a **teaching** ministry. There were miracles (John 2. 23; 3. 2), but they were not made prominent; and the immediate followers of Jesus were won by what they saw in him and heard from him rather than by wonders wrought by him.

VI. Lastly, we ascertain the **Results** of the Saviour's ministry during this period.

1. It gave him **prominence before the people**. The popular attention was arrested, and there was a transient, superficial acceptance by the many; but Jesus knew the hearts of men too well to trust them (John 2. 23, 24; 3. 26).

2. It led to his **rejection by the rulers**. Though this is not stated it is hinted at in the controversies of the Jewish leaders (John 2. 18); in the conclusion of the gospel writer (John 3. 18-20), and in the reference to the Pharisees (John 4. 1). From this hour the attitude of the capital and the ruling minds was hostile to Jesus. They missed the one great opportunity in their nation's history.

3. It drew around him **chosen followers**. From this time there was a company of disciples with Jesus. They returned to their homes in Galilee for a time, but were soon called to leave all and accompany their master. To some of them we find three separate calls (John 1. 37-42; Matt. 4. 18-22 more than a year later, and Mark 3. 13, 14, later still).

4. **It prepared for his ministry in Galilee.** The fame of Christ's acts in Judea went before him to Galilee, awakened curiosity, and gave him a ready reception on his return (John 4. 45). We shall find in the next period great multitudes thronging after Jesus as the result of his ministry in Judea.

Blackboard Outline

I. **Pre. Not.** 1. **Sour. Inf.** Jno. 2. **Ti.** 15 m. 3. **Loc.** Jud. 4. **Aim.** Fir. opp.

II. **Pla.** 1. Beth. 2. Can. 3. Cap. 4. Syc. 5. Jer.

III. **Jour.** 1. W. B. 2. B. C. 3. C. C. 4. C. J. & J. 5. J. S. & C.

IV. **Even.** 1. Fir. Foll. 2. Fir. Mir. 3. Vis. Cap. 4. Fir. Pass. 5. Cle. Tem. 6. Con. Nic. 7. Min. Jud. 8. Min. Sam. 9. Ret. Gal. 10. Heal. Nob. Son.

V. **Gen. Tra.** 1. Prep. 2. Con. J. Bap. 3. Ind. 4. Tea.

VI. **Res.** 1. Prom. 2. Rej. rul. 3. Cho. fol. 4. Prep. Min. Gal.

Questions for Students

What book is our only source of information for this period? How long was the period? Where was it mostly passed? What was Christ's aim at this time? Name the five places of the period, and an event at each. Give in order the ten events of this period. Who were the first six followers of Jesus? What was his first miracle, and where wrought? Where did Jesus go for his first passover? Name two events that took place at this visit. Where did Jesus preach for a time? What led him to another province? Whom did he meet there, and at what place? How long did he stay in the province of Samaria? What were his reasons for returning to Galilee? What miracle did he work on his return? What were the circumstances of this miracle? What were the general traits of Christ's ministry during this period? What were the results of his ministry? How did it prepare the way for his work in Galilee?

SIXTH STUDY

The Year of Popularity

From the Rejection at Nazareth to the Discourse on the Bread of Life

I. General Aspects of the Ministry of Christ during the Period.

1. **Its Time.** It was either a little less or a little more than a year, according to different authorities. According to Dr. Edersheim it extended from May, A. D. 28, to April, A. D. 29; according to Dr. Andrews, from March, A. D. 28, to April, A. D. 29.

2. **Its Locality.** The principal sphere of Christ's activity during this year was Galilee, though he made one visit to Jerusalem (John 5. 1).

3. **Its Aim.** The purpose of Jesus during this year seems to have been to proclaim the new kingdom of God as widely as possible, and to make men acquainted with its principles. The theme of his preaching is given in Matt. 4. 17. The deeper themes of the Gospel were reserved for a later time and a select body of hearers; and those aspects were presented which all men could at once comprehend, as the teaching in the Sermon on the Mount.

4. **Its Activity.** No other year in the Saviour's life was crowded so thickly with journeys and labors. See its summary in Matt. 4. 23-25. We can trace eight distinct journeys from Capernaum to various regions during this year.

5. **Its Divisions.** The number of events left on record makes a subdivision of this period necessary, and we find a convenient place at the Sermon on the Mount, which marks a point of departure in the Saviour's ministry. The **Early Galilean Ministry** extends from the rejection at Nazareth to the Sermon on the Mount, and the **Later Galilean Ministry** from the Sermon on the Mount to the discourse on the Bread of Life. During the earlier section the ministry was personal and the range was less extended; during the later Jesus sent his apostles forth to labor, and his own journeys were longer and in new fields.

II. **The Places.** Though the Saviour visited many places during this year only seven have been named in the gospels. These are:

1. **Capernaum**, his home during the period (Matt. 4. 15). From this place he went forth on all of his preaching tours, and to it he returned. Its privilege (Matt. 11. 23, 24). It was situated on the northwestern shore of the Sea of Galilee.

2. **Nazareth.** Twice in this period Jesus was at this place: at its beginning (Luke 4. 16), and again in the middle of the year (Matt. 13. 54). On both occasions he was rejected by the people (Luke 4. 28, 29; Matt. 13. 57).

3. **Nain.** This was a city southwest of the Sea of Galilee, where Jesus restored a young man to life (Luke 7. 11).

4. **The Mountain.** A few miles from Capernaum and west of the Sea of Galilee is a mountain (probably Kurun Hattin, "the horns of Hattin") where was delivered the Sermon on the Mount (Matt. 5. 1).

5. **Bethsaida**, a place on the northern shore of the Sea of Galilee, east of the river Jordan. Near this was wrought the miracle of Feeding the Five Thousand (Mark 6. 45).

6. **Gergesa.** A place on the eastern shore of the Sea of Galilee, called also **Gerasa** (Mark 5. 1; Luke 8. 26. Rev. Ver.).

7. **Jerusalem.** We read of one visit to the capital during this period (John 5. 1).

III. **The Early Galilean Ministry.**

1.) **The Journeys.** Combining the accounts in the four gospels we find that the journeys were the following:

2.) **The Settlement at Capernaum** (Cana to Nazareth and Capernaum). From Cana, where Jesus was at the close of the preceding period, he went to Nazareth (Luke 4. 16), probably intending to begin his ministry there; but being rejected went down to Capernaum and made it the headquarters of his ministry (Luke 4. 30, 31).

3.) **Tour in Eastern Galilee** (Capernaum, Eastern Galilee, and return). From Capernaum Jesus went forth on a preaching tour through the villages near the Sea of Galilee (Luke 4. 43, 44).

4.) **A Visit to Jerusalem** (Capernaum to Jerusalem and return). Mention is made in John 5. 1 of a feast in Jerusalem which Jesus attended, but it is uncertain whether Passover, Tabernacles, or Purim is meant.

5.) **The Mountain Journey** (Capernaum to the mountain and return). For the purpose of quiet meditation and the call of his apostles Jesus went to a mountain near the Sea of Galilee. There he chose the twelve and gave to them and the multitudes around the Sermon on the Mount (Mark 3. 13, 14; Matt. 5. 1).

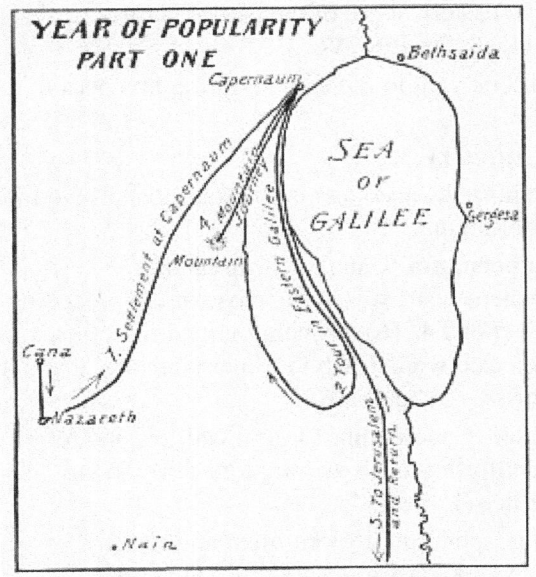

IV. **Events of the Early Galilean Ministry.**

1.) With the first Journey, the *Settlement at Capernaum*, we connect the following events:

1. **The Rejection at Nazareth** (Luke 4. 16-30).
2. **The First Disciples Called** (Luke 5. 1-11). They had already been followers of Jesus, but now were called upon to leave their homes and become his disciples.
3. **Miracles at Capernaum** (Mark 1. 21-34). The gospel writers select the scenes of one day and show many miracles, in the synagogue, at Peter's house, and in the street.

2.) With the Second Journey, the *Tour in Eastern Galilee*, we find two events named:

4. **Healing of the Leper** (Mark 1. 40-45). This took place during the journey.
5. **Healing the Paralytic** (Mark 2. 1-12). This took place after the return to Capernaum.

3.) With the Third Journey, the *Visit to Jerusalem*, we note two events:

6. **The Miracle at Bethesda** (John 5. 1-16). Read this in the Rev. Ver. and note what is omitted. Observe also what resulted from this miracle in Jerusalem (John 5. 16-19).
7. **The Withered Hand** (Mark 3. 1-6). This probably took place at Capernaum, soon after the return from Jerusalem.

4.) With the Fourth, the *Mountain Journey*, we note two events:

8. **The Call of the Twelve** (Mark 3. 7-19). This was at the mountain.

9. **Sermon on the Mount** (Matt. 5-7). This sermon is omitted in Mark and abbreviated in Luke, but reported fully in Matthew.

To the Teacher

1. Let the outline of the lesson be committed to memory.

2. Let one scholar draw the maps in presence of the class, another insert the places, a third indicate and name the journeys.

3. Then let one scholar name all the events with the first journey; another the events of the second journey, etc.

4. Let a scholar be called upon to tell the story of each one of the nine events in the period.

Blackboard Outline
Part One

I. **Gen. Asp.** 1. Ti. 2. Loc. 3. Aim. 4. Act. 5. Div.

II. **Pla.** 1. Cap. 2. Naz. 3. Nai. 4. Moun. 5. Beth. 6. Ger. 7. Jer.

III. **Ear. Gal. Min. Jour.** 1. Set. Cap. 2. To. Ea. Gal. 3. Vis. Jer. 4. Moun. I. Jour.

IV. **Events. Ear. Gal. Min.**

Jour. 1. 1. Rej Naz. 2. Fir. Dis. Cal. 3. Mir. Cap.

Jour. 2. 4. Heal Lep. 5. Heal Par.

Jour. 3. 6. Mir. Beth. 7. With. Ha.

Jour. 4. 8. Ca. Tw. 9. Ser. Mo.

Questions for Review

Part One

How long was this period? Where was it passed? What was the aim of Jesus during this year? What are its two subdivisions? Name seven places visited by Jesus during this period. Name four journeys during the early part of this period. What three events are connected with the settlement at Capernaum? What two events are named in connection with the tour in eastern Galilee? What two events are given with the visit to Jerusalem? What two events are named with the mountain journey?

Part Two

We now take up the second part of the Year of Popularity, from the Sermon on the Mount to the Discourse on the Bread of Life.

V. **The Journeys of the Later Galilean Ministry.**

1. **Tour in Southern Galilee** (Capernaum to Nain and return). From Capernaum Jesus led his disciples southward as far as Nain (Luke 7. 1, 11). There he wrought a miracle, and on the journey homeward preached in various places (Luke 8. 1).

2. **The Voyage to Gergesa.** (Capernaum to Gergesa and return.) With his disciples Jesus sailed across the Sea of Galilee (Luke 8. 22), stilling the tempest on the way. They landed at Gergesa, in the country of the Gadarenes (Luke 8. 26)—that is, not far from the well-known city of Gadara, which was twenty miles from the Sea of Galilee. Here the Gadarene demoniac was restored, but the people were unwilling to receive Jesus, so he sailed back to Capernaum (Matt. 9. 1.)

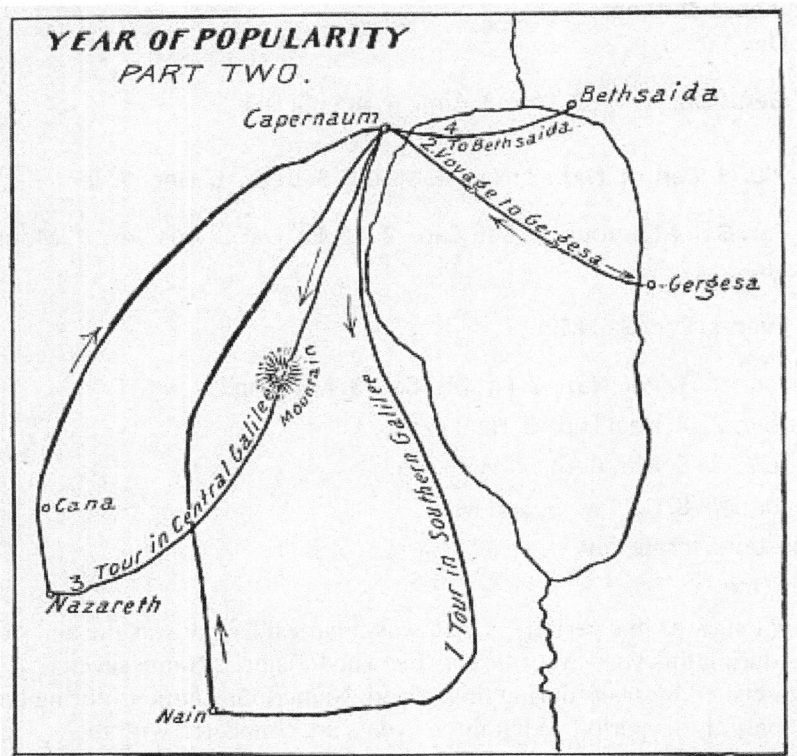

3. **Tour in Central Galilee** (Capernaum to Nazareth and return). The object of this journey was a second visit to Nazareth (Mark 6. 1), but,

like the first, it was unsuccessful; so Jesus left "his own country" and preached in the villages of central Galilee (Mark 6. 6).

4. **Retirement to Bethsaida** (Capernaum, Bethsaida, and return). In order to obtain needed rest and seclusion Jesus and his disciples sailed across the lake to the unsettled country near Bethsaida (Mark 6. 31, 32). Here he wrought the miracle of Feeding the Five Thousand, recrossed the lake in the night, and a day or two afterward gave his last discourse of the Galilean ministry.

Let the pupil draw the same map as with Part One, but omitting the journeys of that part; and place upon the maps the journeys of the later Galilean ministry.

VI. The Events of the Later Galilean Ministry.

1.) With the First Journey, the *Tour in Southern Galilee*:

1.) **The Widow's Son Raised** (Luke 7. 11-16). This took place at Nain, southwest of the Sea of Galilee.

2.) **Washing the Saviour's Feet** (Luke 7. 36-50). This event is to be carefully distinguished from the "anointing by Mary," much later in the history.

These two events are related only by Luke.

2.) With the Second Journey, the *Voyage to Gergesa*:

3.) **Parables by the Sea** (Mark 4. 1-34; also in Matt. 13. 1-52). These were given just before the journey.

4.) **Stilling the Tempest** (Mark 4. 1-35-41).

5.) **The Gadarene Demoniac Restored** (Mark 5. 1-20).

6.) **Jairus's Daughter Raised** (Mark 5. 21-43). Two miracles wrought after the return from the Gadarene country.

3.) With the third Journey, the *Tour in Central Galilee*.

7.) **Second Rejection at Nazareth** (Mark 6. 1-6). Compare with this the account of his former rejection, and note the differences.

8.) **Sending out the Twelve** (Mark 6. 7-13). Read the longer report of the charge to the Twelve in Matt. 10.

4.) With the Fourth Journey, the *Retirement to Bethsaida*:

9.) **Feeding the Five Thousand** (Mark 6. 31-44). This and the following are the only miracles related in all the four gospels. Compare their accounts.

10.) **Walking on the Sea** (Mark 6. 45-52). Note the additions in Matt. 14. 22-33).

11.) **Discourse on the Bread of Life** (John 6. 24-59). This marked a crisis in his ministry, for it proclaimed a spiritual application of the miracle, and not a "kingdom of meat and drink," as men were expecting. Note the results (John 6. 60-68). Thus at the close of his Galilean ministry—as before at the close of his Judean ministry—the Saviour was left alone with his few disciples.

Blackboard Outline
Part Two

V. **Jour. Lat. Gal. Min.** 1. To. Gal. 2. Voy. Ger. 3. To. Cen. Gal. 4. Ret. Beth.

VI. **Ev. Lat. Gal. Min.—**

Jour. 1. 1. Wid. So. Rai. 2. Wash. Sav. Fe.
Jour. 2. 3. Par. Sea. 4. Still Tem. 5. Gad. Dem. Res. 6. Jai. Dau. Ra.
Jour. 3. 7. Sec. Rej. Naz. 8. Sen. Twel.
Jour. 4. 9. Fe. Fi. Th. 10 Wal. Sea. 11. Dis. Br. Li.

Questions for Review
Part Two

How many journeys are named with the later Galilean ministry? What was the first journey of the later Galilean ministry? The second journey? The third? The fourth? What two events took place with the tour in southern Galilee? What four events with the Gadarene voyage? What two events with the tour in Central Galilee? What three events with the retirement to Bethsaida?

SEVENTH STUDY

The Year of Opposition

From the Retirement to Phœnicia to the Anointing by Mary

Part One

I. **General Aspects of the Period.**

1. **It was a year, lacking one week.** Jesus did not attend the third passover of his ministry. We find him at this time still in Galilee, and

soon afterward leaving Galilee for "the coasts of Tyre and Sidon" (John 7. 1-3; Mark 7. 24). Nearly a year later, on the week before the fourth passover, we find Jesus at Bethany, where the anointing by Mary took place (John 12. 1, 2). Between these two passovers came the year of opposition.

2. **It was a year of wandering.** During this period we notice that Jesus was in constant motion, staying only a little while at each place, and in succession visiting all the five provinces of Palestine. Notice the province referred to in each of the following references: John 7. 1; Mark 7. 31; Mark 8. 27; Luke 9. 51, 52; Mark 10. 1; John 10. 40.

3. **It was a year of retirement.** We do not find that Jesus sought the multitudes during this year, though in new places he was sought by them (Luke 11. 29; 12. 1). He seems to have chosen most of the time a secluded life, preferring to be alone with his disciples. See instances in Mark 7. 24, 32, 33, 36; 8. 22, 23, 26; 9. 30.

4. **It was a year of instruction.** He chose to be alone with his disciples, knowing that he was rapidly nearing the close of his life on earth; and he wished to instruct his chosen followers in the deeper truths of the gospel before he should be taken from them. His teaching in this period presented the spiritual side of truth and the doctrines of the cross. Notice how often during this year he foretold his own death (Mark 8. 31; 9. 31, 32; 10. 32-34; John 12. 7, 8).

5. **It was a year of opposition.** Nearly all the people had now forsaken Jesus and turned against him. Note the attitude of the Pharisees. (Matt 12. 23, 24, 38, 39; 23. 23.) The Sadducees, who were the office-holding class, are mainly referred to in John 11. 47, 48, 53. The attitude of the people. (John 6. 66.) Jesus was now rejected by the rulers, the leaders of the religious class, and by the people.

II. **The Localities of the Period.** Beside the five provinces, Judea, Samaria, Galilee, Bashan and Peræa, two other lands or districts are named:

1. **Phœnicia**, called in the gospels "the borders of Tyre and Sidon," narrow strip of territory between Mount Lebanon and the Mediterranean Sea, northwest of Palestine.

2. **Decapolis.** The word means "ten cities," and refers to a region, partly in Bashan and partly in Peræa, wherein were ten important cities, not Jewish but Gentile.

In addition to the above we meet with names of eight cities:

3. **Cæsarea Philippi**, at the foot of Mount Hermon, in the province of Bashan.

4. **Bethsaida**, on the northeastern shore of the Sea of Galilee.

5. **Capernaum**, on the northwestern shore of the Sea of Galilee.

6. **Bethabara**, in the Jordan Valley, east of the river, south of the Sea of Galilee.

7. **Jericho**, in the Jordan Valley, west of the river, near the head of the Dead Sea.

8. **Jerusalem**, the capital.

9. **Bethany**, two miles east of Jerusalem, on the eastern slope of the Mount of Olives.

10. **Ephraim**, or Ephron, fourteen miles north of Jerusalem, among the mountains.

III. **The Journeys and Events of the Period.** The information upon this year is meager, and it is impossible to arrange its places and facts with absolute certainty. No other period is so uncertain in the order of its events as this. We trace in this period nine journeys; and with each journey call attention to the most important events connected with it. The first journey begins at Capernaum.

1. **A Visit to Phœnicia.** (From Capernaum to Phœnicia.) (Matt. 15. 21). This was the only land outside of Palestine visited by Jesus, and it is uncertain how far he entered within its limits. He sought retirement and opportunity of instructing his disciples (Mark 7. 24).

On this journey was wrought the miracle on the **Syrophenician Woman's Daughter** (Mark 7. 25, 26), in which Jesus showed his disciples that Gentiles may have true faith.

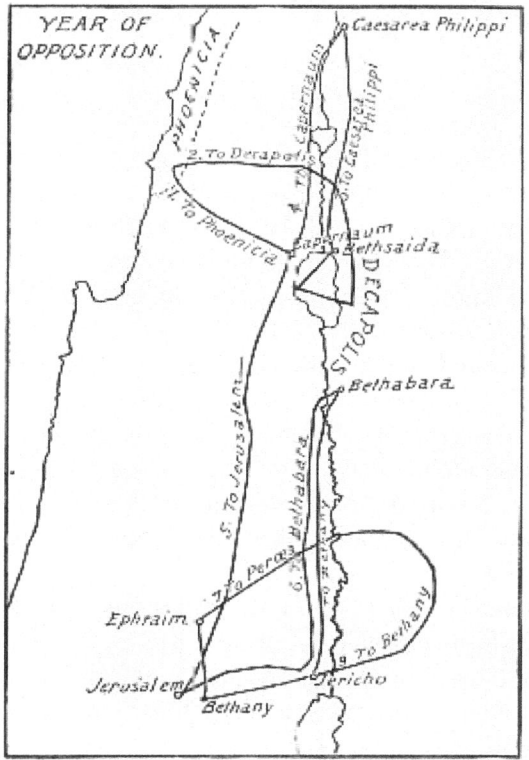

2. **A Visit to Decapolis.** Finding seclusion impossible he went around Galilee to Decapolis, east of the Sea of Galilee (Mark 7. 31).

Here two miracles were wrought: 1.) **Healing the Deaf Man.** Notice its peculiarities in Mark 7. 32-37. 2.) **Feeding the Four Thousand** (Mark 8. 1-9). Notice its differences from a former miracle in the preceding period.

3. **A Visit to Cæsarea Philippi.** (Decapolis to Dalmanutha, Bethsaida, and Cæsarea Philippi.) Trace the route from Mark 8. 10, 22, 27.

During this journey occurred four events: 1.) **Healing the Blind Man** (Mark 8. 22-26). This was at Bethsaida. 2.) **Peter's Confession** (Matt. 16. 13-20). 3.) **The Transfiguration** (Mark 9. 2-8). 4.) **Healing the Demoniac Boy** (Mark 9. 14-29). These three events were at Cæsarea Philippi.

4. **A Visit to Capernaum.** (Cæsarea Philippi to Capernaum.) (Mark 9. 33). Notice that his coming was unattended by the crowds of former times (Mark 9. 33). This visit is noteworthy as his farewell to the city which had been his home.

On this visit took place the touching incident of the **Child in the Midst** (Mark 9. 36, 37).

Part Two

5. **A Visit to Jerusalem.** (Capernaum, through Samaria, to Jerusalem.) See Luke 9. 51, 52. His visit to the capital was for the purpose of attending the Feast of Tabernacles (John 7. 2, 10, 14) and he seems to have remained until the Feast of Dedication, two months later.

In connection with this visit note, 1.) **The Rejection by Samaritans** (Luke 9. 52-56). 2.) **Mary and Martha** (Luke 10. 38-42). 3.) **The Pool of Siloam** (John 9. 1-7). 4.) **The Good Shepherd** (John 10. 1-18).

6. **A Visit to Bethabara.** (Jerusalem to Bethabara.) From the Feast of Dedication Jesus went down to Bethabara, evidently with the purpose of beginning a ministry in Peræa (John 10. 39, 40).

With this journey we place **Sending out the Seventy** (Luke 10. 1). These messengers were sent out to prepare for the visit of Jesus to a new province.

7. **A Visit to Bethany** (John 11. 1, 7.) From Bethabara Jesus was suddenly called to Bethany, near Jerusalem (John 11. 18).

With this visit we place the **Raising of Lazarus** (John 11. 1-46), a miracle narrated only by John, and told because it led directly to the conspiracy against the life of Jesus (John 11. 47, 48).

8. **A Visit to Peræa.** (From Bethany to Ephraim and Peræa.) Trace the journey from John 11. 54, and Mark 10. 1. Jesus stayed some months in Peræa, preaching to his people.

Many events might be given with this Peræan ministry, of which we name only, 1.) **Blessing the Children** (Mark 10. 13-16). 2.) **The Rich Young Ruler** (Mark 10. 17-25). 3.) **Parable of the Prodigal Son** (Luke 15. 11-32).

9. **A Second Visit to Bethany.** (From Peræa, through Jericho, to Bethany.) Notice the journey in Mark 10. 32, 46; John 12. 1.

With this journey notice the events, 1.) **The Healing of Bartimæus** (Mark 10. 46, 52). 2.) **The Visit to Zacchæus** (Luke 19. 1-10). 3.) **The Anointing by Mary** (John 12. 1-8). This brings the life of Christ within one week of the Crucifixion, and completes the period.

Blackboard Outline

I. **Gen. Asp.** 1. Year. 2. Wan. 3. Ret. 4. Ins. 5. Opp.

II. **Loc. Per.** La. Ph. Dec. Cit. C. P. B. C. B. J. J. B. E.

II I. **Jour.** 1. **Vis. Phœ.** 1.) Syr. Wom. Dau.

   2. **Vis. Dec.** 1.) He. De. M. 2.) Fe. Fou. Thou.

   3. **Vis. Ces. Phil.** 1.) Hea. Bl. M. 2.) Pet. Con. 3.) Trans. 4.) Hea. Dem. B.

   4. **Vis. Cap.** 1.) Ch. Mid.

   5. **Vis. Jer.** 1.) Rej. Sam. 2.) M. and M. 3.) P. Sil. 4.) G. Sh.

   6. **Vis. Beth.** 1.) Sen. 70.

   7. **Vis. Beth.** 1.) Rai. Laz.

   8. **Vis. Per.** 1.) Bl. Ch. 2.) R. Yo. Ru. 3.) Par. Prod. So.

   9. **Sec. Vis. Beth.** 1.) Hea. Bar. 2.) Vis. Zac. 3.) Anoin. Ma.

Review Questions

With what event does the Year of Opposition begin? With what does it end? How long was it? Where was it passed? How did it differ from the preceding year? Why did Jesus seek retirement at this time? What was the feeling of the people toward Jesus? What land outside of Palestine was visited by Jesus? What miracle was wrought during this visit? Where was the Second Journey of this Period? What two miracles were wrought at this time? What was the Third Journey? Name four events connected with this journey. What was the Fourth Journey? The Fifth Journey? Name four events with this journey. Where did Jesus go for the Sixth Journey? Whom did he send out at this time, and for what purpose? What was the place and what the purpose of the Seventh Journey? Where was the Eighth Journey? What took place with this journey? What was the Ninth Journey? Name three events of this journey.

EIGHTH STUDY

The Week of the Passion

From the Triumphal Entry Until the Agony in the Garden

I. **General View of the Period.**

1. Our studies have now reached the close of the Saviour's ministry and have brought us to his **last visit to Jerusalem**. This period presents the last appeal of Jesus to the Jewish people and his final conversations with his disciples before his death.

2. Strictly speaking, "the week of the passion" or suffering of Jesus should include all the events from his Triumphal Entry into Jerusalem on Sunday until his burial on Friday evening. But the events of the day of his crucifixion were so many and so important as to make that day a period by itself, and we therefore consider at present only **five days**, from the Sunday morning to the Thursday night of the Jewish Passover, the night before the Saviour's crucifixion.

3. All its events took place in or **near Jerusalem**. On each morning Jesus went from Bethany, where he remained at night with his friends, the household of Mary and Martha; and on each evening except the last he returned to Bethany. The days were mostly spent in Jerusalem.

II. In the study of this period we note the following **Places**:

1. **Bethany**, a small village on the eastern slope of the Mount of Olives. It was the home of Mary, Martha, and Lazarus (John 11. 1). Its distance from Jerusalem (John 11. 18). The lodging place of Jesus at this time (Matt. 21. 17).

2. **The Temple** in Jerusalem. Here Jesus passed most of the time during the first three days of this week in discussion with the Jews (Luke 21. 37). The part of the temple in which Jesus taught (John 8. 20; Mark 12. 41). This was the Court of the Women, called "the treasury" because of boxes for contributions upon its walls. It was inside the larger Court of the Gentiles, and was about two hundred and thirty feet square, open above to the sky, but with galleries around.

3. **The Supper room.** See Mark 14. 13-17. The place is unknown; but there is on Mount Zion a locality pointed out by tradition which may or may not be correct. This was probably the "upper room" used as a meeting place after the Resurrection and Ascension (John 20. 19; Acts 1. 13; 2. 1).

4. **The Mount of Olives.** This is a range of hills east of Jerusalem and separated from the Temple by the Valley of the Kedron (John 18. 1). Its distance from the city (Acts 1. 12). Here began the Triumphal Entry (Luke 19. 37). From this height Jesus gave his prophecy of the destruction of the city (Mark 13. 3, 4).

5. **The Garden of Gethsemane.** The word means "oil-press," and suggests that it was an olive orchard on the western slope of the Mount of Olives (Mark 14. 26, 32). A garden is still shown which may be the true locality of the Agony.

Let the student draw a map of Jerusalem and its surroundings and locate upon it the above places, not failing to search out the references and associate the events with their localities.

III. We draw on our map and fix in our memory the following **Journeys**:

1. **On Sunday, the First Journey; from Bethany to the Temple and Return.** On the first day of the week Jesus left Bethany, entered in triumphal procession into Jerusalem, looked around on the Temple, and at evening returned to Bethany.

2. **On Monday, the Second Journey; from Bethany to the Temple and Return.** Early in the morning, without waiting for breakfast, Jesus left Bethany (Mark 11. 12), and crossed the ridge of the Mount of Olives, on the way cursing the barren fig tree. He cleansed the Temple of its traders, and at evening returned again to Bethany (Mark 11. 19).

3. **On Tuesday, the Third Journey; from Bethany to the Temple and Return.** This was the last day of Christ's public teaching, closing with a terrible denunciation of the Scribes and Pharisees. Toward evening he went out of the Temple for the last time, sat upon the Mount of Olives with his disciples, and gave to them his prediction of the destruction of the city (Mark 13. 1-4).

4. **On Thursday afternoon, the Fourth Journey; from Bethany to the Supper room.** Take notice that no journey or event is named by any evangelist as taking place on Wednesday. Probably the day was passed in seclusion and meditation, for no conversations with disciples are recorded. On Thursday afternoon Jesus with his disciples left Bethany and walked over the mountain and the valley to Jerusalem (Mark 14. 16, 17), where they celebrated the passover and partook of the Last Supper together. Afterward came the long conversations recorded in John 13 to 17.

5. **On Thursday, at about midnight, the Fifth Journey; from the Supper room to Gethsemane.** The Saviour and his eleven disciples went from the supper room into the silent streets of Jerusalem, through the gate, and into the valley of Kedron. They crossed the brook and entered the Garden of Gethsemane, where the Agony took place, and immediately after it the Arrest (John 18. 1).

IV. We now pass in order the **Events** of these five days:

1. **The Triumphal Entry.** (Sunday.) (Mark 11. 1-10.) Compare the accounts and note the additions made by John. (John 12. 12-16.)

2. **The Barren Fig tree.** (Monday.) (Mark 11. 12-14.) This was not a wanton or petulant act of cursing. The tree was a vivid picture of the Jewish state, bearing leaves but no fruit, and the miracle was wrought as a warning of impending doom.

3. **Cleansing the Temple.** (Monday.) (Mark 11. 15-17.) Once before, in the beginning of his ministry, Jesus had purged the Temple (John 2.

13-16). But the former abuses had crept in again, and Christ again proclaimed his authority in his Father's house.

4. **The Last Discourses.** (Tuesday.) (Mark 11. 27; 12. 44.) On this day Jesus met and vanquished in debate successively the rulers (Mark 11. 27-33); the Pharisees (Mark 12. 1-12; Matt. 21. 45); the Herodians (Mark 12. 13-17); the Sadducees (Mark 12. 18-27); and the scribes (Mark 12. 28-37). He closed his ministry with a rebuke to the scribes and Pharisees (Matt. 23. 1-39); and after commending the gift of the widow (Mark 12. 41-44) went out of the Temple, never to return (Mark 13. 1, 2.)

5. **The Prophecy of the Last Things.** (Tuesday.) In the afternoon of that day Jesus sat with his disciples on the Mount of Olives, and looking down upon the city gave a prophecy to his disciples, mingling the predictions of the city's overthrow and of the end of the world (Mark 13. 1-37). In Matthew are added two parables—the Ten Virgins (Matt. 25. 1-13), and the Talents (Matt. 25. 14-30), and also the description of the Last Judgment (Matt. 25. 31-46).

6. **The Retirement at Bethany.** (Wednesday.) Inasmuch as none of the gospels mention any event of Wednesday we assume that the day was passed in retirement.

7. **The Last Supper.** (Thursday.) On the afternoon of Thursday Jesus went to Jerusalem with the Twelve, partook of the Passover, and at its close instituted the Lord's Supper (Mark 14. 12-31).

8. **The Last Conversation.** (Thursday evening.) (John 14 to 18.) After the Supper the long conversation took place recorded in full by John, and scarcely mentioned in the other gospels.

9. **The Agony in the Garden.** (Thursday, midnight.) Late at night Jesus crossed the brook Kedron and entered the Garden of Gethsemane, where the Agony came upon him (Mark 14. 32-42).

Blackboard Outline
The Week of the Passion

I. **Gen. Vi.** 1. La. Vis. Jer. 2. Fi. Da. 3. Ne. Jer.

II **Pla.** 1. Beth. 2. Tem. 3. Sup.-ro. 4. Mo. Oli. 5. Gar. Geth.

II **Jour.** 1. (Sun.) Be. Tem. Re. 2. (Mon.) Be. Tem. Re. 3. (Tu.) Be. I. Tem. Re. 4. (Thu.) Be. Sup.-ro. 5. (Thu.) Sup.-ro. Geth.

I **Events.** 1. Tri. Ent. (Sun.) 2. Bar. Fig. tr. (Mon.) 3. Cl. Tem. (Mon.) V. 4. La. Dis. (Tue.) 5. Pro. La. Th. (Tue.) 6. Ret. Beth. (Wed.) 7. La. Sup. (Thu.) 8. La. Con. (Thu.) 9. Ag. Gar. (Thu.)

Questions for Review

Where did the events of this period take place? Between what days did they occur? In what village did Jesus pass most of the nights of this week? Where was the Last Supper partaken? Where did Jesus begin his triumphal entry into the city? What journey took place on the Sunday of this week? On Monday? On Tuesday? On Thursday afternoon? Name the events of Sunday. Of Monday. Of Tuesday. Of Wednesday. Of Thursday.

NINTH STUDY

The Day of the Crucifixion

From the Betrayal to the Burial of Jesus

I. General View of the Period.

1. This period embraces the events of but **one day** in the life of Jesus. It was the day following the Passover Day, and therefore the fifteenth of the month Nisan, in the Jewish year. See Num. 28. 16.

The betrayal of Jesus took place a little after midnight, on Friday morning, and the burial about sunset on the same day; so that the transactions of the period include about eighteen hours.

2. It was, however, **an eventful day** in the life of Jesus. No day in all Bible story is narrated with the fullness of this day. Nearly one-twelfth of the matter in the four gospels is occupied with the account of this one day. If the whole story of Christ's life were written out with equal completeness to this one day's record it would require more than four hundred volumes as large as the New Testament.

3. It was an **important day**; the most important in the history of the world. Notice in the epistles how much more is said of the death of Christ than of his life. See 1 Cor. 2. 2; Gal. 6. 14; 1 John 1. 7. Because of its eventfulness and importance we should give it careful study and place in order its events as a separate period in the life of Jesus Christ.

II. **The Places.** All these are in or near Jerusalem; but none of them can be identified with certainty. Yet it is well to know the traditional localities and to fix them upon the map of the city. There are five places named in the story of this day.

1. **The Garden of Gethsemane.** Here Jesus was arrested, immediately after the agony (Mark 14. 43). See the mention of this locality in the last study.

2. **The High Priest's House** (Mark 14. 53, 54). The high priest at that time was Caiaphas, but his father-in-law, Annas, who had been deposed

by the Romans, was still regarded by the Jews as the legitimate priest, and possessed great authority. There was no special "palace" of the high priest, and Annas and Caiaphas may have lived in the same group of buildings. The place is located by tradition on Mount Zion, near that of the supper room.

3. **Pilate's Palace** (Mark 15. 1-16). The Roman capital of Judea was not in Jerusalem, but at Cæsarea, where the procurator resided (Acts 23. 23, 24). But it was customary for the governor to visit Jerusalem at the time of Passover, in order to quell any disturbance at that time, when the city was thronged. Pilate may have made his headquarters in Jerusalem either in the castle of Antonia, north of the temple (referred to in Acts 21. 34, and elsewhere), or in the palace of Herod the Great on the northwest corner of Mount Zion, the place now occupied by the (so-called) Tower of David. The latter locality is accepted by the best of the recent authorities. Here Jesus was brought for his trial and sentence by Pontius Pilate.

4. **Herod's Palace.** At that time Herod Antipas, tetrarch of Galilee and Peræa (Luke 3. 1), the slayer of John the Baptist, was present in Jerusalem attending the Passover, and to him Jesus was sent by Pilate (Luke 23. 7). His abiding place was probably the old Maccabean palace, about midway between the temple and Pilate's headquarters.

5. **Calvary or Golgotha.** See Luke 23. 33 and Mark 15. 22 for the two names, one of which is Greek, the other Hebrew, both meaning "skull-like" or "the place of skulls." All positively known about this place is that it was outside the wall, but near the city (John 19. 20). Two localities are given: the traditional one, north of Zion and west of the temple, now occupied by the Church of the Holy Sepulcher; the other, recently coming into notice and accepted by many scholars, a hill on the north of the city, containing a great cave known as the "Grotto of Jeremiah." We adopt the latter place as Calvary, although the evidence is by no means certain. The place of the cross and that of the burial were in the same locality (John 19. 41, 42).

It would be well for the student to draw a rough diagram showing these places in their general relation to each other, as above.

III. We notice the **Journeys of Jesus** on the day of his crucifixion.

1. **From Gethsemane to the High Priest's House.** From the Garden of Gethsemane Jesus was taken to the high priest's house for examination before Annas and Caiaphas (Luke 22. 54.)

2. **From the High Priest's House to Pilate's Palace.** After examination before the high priests and the Jewish council Jesus was led to Pilate for another trial (Luke 23. 1).

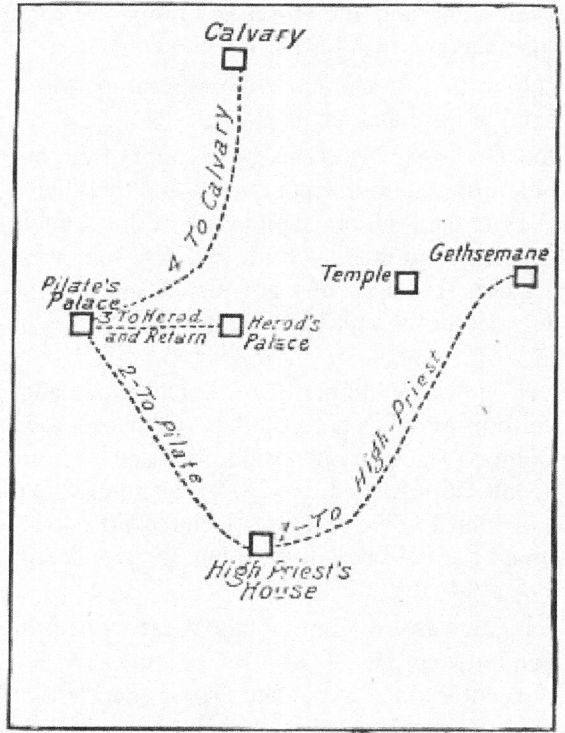

3. **From Pilate's Palace to Herod's Palace and return.** Pilate sent Jesus to Herod Antipas, tetrarch of Galilee; but Herod was unwilling to pass judgment upon him and sent him back (Luke 23. 7-11).

4. **From Pilate's Palace to Calvary.** At this second appearance before Pilate Jesus was condemned to death, and was taken to Calvary, outside the wall. Here he was crucified and after his death was buried (John 19. 16, 17, 41).

Let the student draw on the diagram a line representing each of these journeys and recall the events associated with them.

In Jerusalem, at the present time, there is a street known as Via Dolorosa, "the Sorrowful Way," over which Jesus is believed to have carried his cross from Pilate's judgment hall to Calvary. But in our view both Pilate's judgment hall and Calvary are wrongly located by tradition, and therefore this path cannot be the true "way of the cross."

IV. **The Events.** We may group all the transactions of this momentous day around eleven leading events:

1. **The Betrayal** (Mark 14. 43-50). This was in the Garden of Gethsemane, a little after midnight, and, therefore, on Friday, the 15th of Nisan. See the more detailed account in John 18. 1-11.

2. **Jesus before Annas** (John 18. 12, 13). This was a preliminary examination, and not official in its character.

3. **Jesus before Caiaphas** (John 18. 24). Read the account of the event in Mark 14. 53-72. By comparing the four accounts we find that there was first an examination before the high priest and such of the council as could be gathered (Mark 14. 55), and then later a trial before the entire Sanhedrin, or body of the elders (Luke 22. 66), at which Jesus was condemned to death. Peter's denial took place in the house of the high priest (John 18. 24, 25).

4. **Jesus before Pilate.** The Jews had no power to sentence to death, and hence were compelled to bring Jesus before Pilate (John 18. 28-32). Notice that the Jews condemned Jesus on one ground, but accused him before Pilate on another (Matt. 26. 65, 66; Luke 23. 2). The dialogue of Pilate with Jesus is given in John 18. 29-37. Pilate declared Christ's innocence and proposed that he should be released, but the people still demanded that he should be put to death.

5. **Jesus before Herod.** Pilate was unwilling to take the responsibility either of putting to death an innocent man or of offending the Jews by releasing him. He therefore sent him to Herod. But Herod also refused to judge the case and after mocking Jesus sent him back to Pilate (Luke 23. 6-11).

6. **Jesus Condemned to Death.** After Jesus was brought back Pilate still endeavored to save his life. But instead of setting him free at once as an innocent man he proposed to release him as an act of good feeling at the Passover festival. The Jews chose Barabbas and rejected Jesus; and at last Pilate gave unwilling sentence that Jesus should be crucified. He was then delivered to the soldiers to be mocked and tortured (Luke 23. 13-25).

7. **Jesus Bearing his Cross.** On the way from Pilate's palace to Calvary Jesus was compelled to carry one of the beams of his own cross (John 19. 17). A part of the way his cross was carried by a man named Simon, of Cyrene, in Africa (Mark 15. 21).

8. **Jesus on the Cross.** At Calvary Jesus was fastened to the cross by nails through his hands and feet (Luke 23. 33; John 20. 25). He was crucified at nine o'clock in the morning and lived until three o'clock in the afternoon (Mark 15. 25-34). The stupefying potion offered to him

before he was crucified (Mark 15. 23). Note the four versions of the superscription (Matt. 27. 37; Mark 15. 26; Luke 23. 38; John 19. 19). The witnesses (John 19. 25).

9. **The Seven Words from the Cross.** The first word (Luke 23. 34). The second word (John 19. 26, 27). The third word (Luke 23. 43). The fourth word (Matt. 27. 46). The fifth word (John 19. 28). The sixth word (John 19. 30). The seventh word (Luke 23. 46).

10. **The Death on the Cross.** The fact (Mark 15. 37). A remarkable testimony (Mark 15. 39). A remarkable event (Matt. 27. 51-53). An evidence of his death (John 19. 32-35).

11. **The Burial.** Why the body was taken away (John 19. 31). How it was obtained (John 19. 38). The preparation (John 19. 39, 40). The place of burial (Matt. 27. 59, 60). The witnesses (Matt. 27. 61). The sealing of the tomb (Matt. 27. 62-66).

Blackboard Outline
Day of Crucifixion

I. **Gen. Vie.** 1. On. Da. 2. Ev. Da. 3. Imp. Da.

II **Pla.** 1. Gar. Geth. 2. H. P. Ho. 3. Pil. Pal. 4. Her. Pal. 5. Cal. Gol.

II **Jour.** 1. Geth. H.-p. Ho. 2. H.-p Ho. Pil. Pal. 3. Pil. Pal. Her. Pal. Re. I. 4. Pil. Pal. Calv.

I **Events.** 1. Betr. 2. J. bef. Ann. 3. J. bef. Cai. 4. J. bef. Pil. 5. J. bef. V. Her. 6. J. Con. Dea. 7. J. Bear. Cro. 8. J. on Cro. 9. Sev. Wo. Cro. 10. De. Cro. 11. Bur.

Questions for Review

How long was this period? What was its date in the Jewish year? What shows that it was an eventful day? Why was this the most important day in the world's history? What are the five places named in this period? State the probable location of each place. Name four journeys of this period. Name eleven events of this period. Before what rulers was Jesus brought for examination or trial? State the seven utterances of Jesus on the cross. What took place at the moment of Jesus's death? Why was the body buried so soon? Why was the tomb sealed? Who witnessed the burial?

TENTH STUDY

The Forty Days of Resurrection

From the Resurrection to the Ascension of Christ

I. **The Necessity of Christ's Resurrection.** Strange as the resurrection may appear to men in general, and unexpected as it was to the disciples of Jesus, it was the necessary completion of his work on earth.

1. It was necessary **from the nature of Christ**. A divine man, it was impossible that he should be held in the grave (Acts 2. 24). His resurrection showed that he was the Son of God (Rom. 1. 4).

2. It was necessary **for the fulfillment of prophecy**. Jesus himself declared that the prophecies pointed to his resurrection (Luke 24. 45, 46). The apostles constantly appealed to the Old Testament prophecies (Acts 13. 34, 35; 26. 22, 23; 1 Cor. 15. 4).

3. It was necessary for the **work of redemption**. He lived as our example, and he must appear before God as our high priest and mediator (Rom. 4. 25; 8. 34; 1 Cor. 15. 17).

4. It was necessary for the **faith of the disciples**. If Christ had not risen the world would never have heard of his life and the church would never have existed (1 Cor. 15. 19, 20; 1 Pet. 1. 3).

5. It was necessary to **attest Christ's authority**. But for the resurrection the name of Jesus could have possessed no more weight than any other name. Raised from the dead he has all power (Matt. 28. 18; Acts 13. 33; 17. 31).

6. It was necessary as a **pledge of our resurrection**. If Christ rose we too shall rise (Acts 26. 23; 1 Cor. 15. 12, 20-23).

II. **The Fact of Christ's Resurrection.**

1. **It was proved by the testimony of witnesses.** See Acts 1. 3; 2. 32. The conduct of the disciples before and after the resurrection was in itself a proof. Before they were in sorrow (Mark 16. 10; Luke 24. 17). Afterward they were glad (Luke 24. 52; John 20. 20). The Christian Church to-day is the best evidence; for without the resurrection it could never have been established.

2. **It was effected by the power of God.** (Acts 3. 15; Rom. 8. 11; Eph. 1. 20). Jesus speaks of his own power in connection with this (John 2. 19; 10. 18). The Holy Spirit is also mentioned as raising Christ from the dead (1 Peter 3. 18).

3. It took place **on the first day of the week.** (Mark 16. 9). In commemoration of this event the first day of the week was observed by

the early Church (Acts 20. 7; 1 Cor. 16. 2). The name given to this day (Rev. 1. 10).

4. It took place on **the third day after his death**. The body of Jesus was in the grave between thirty and thirty-six hours—from sunset on Friday to daybreak on Sunday. But in the Jewish notation of time this was three days (Luke 24. 46; Acts 10. 40; 1 Cor. 15. 4).

III. **The Ten Appearances of Jesus after his Resurrection.** It is not easy, perhaps not possible, to harmonize precisely all the accounts in the gospels and in 1 Cor. 15. 4-7. But the best authorities unite in the following order of the manifestations of Christ between the resurrection and the ascension:

1. **To Mary Magdalene** (Mark 16. 9). This was at the sepulcher, very soon after the resurrection. Several women went to the sepulcher, found it open, and were told by an angel that Jesus had risen. They went to bear the news to the disciples (Mark 16. 1-8; Matt. 28. 1-8; Luke 24. 1-10). Mary Magdalene returned after the rest had gone and saw the risen Lord (John 20. 1-18). Notice that this Mary is to be carefully distinguished from Mary of Bethany, John 11. 2, and from the unnamed woman in Luke 7. 37.

2. **To the other women** (Matt. 28. 9). This was near the sepulcher, a few minutes later than the first appearance. The names of these women (Mark 16. 1; Luke 24. 10).

3. **To two disciples** (Luke 24. 13-32). The place where Jesus was revealed (Luke 24. 13). The name of Luke's probable informant (Luke 24. 18).

4. **To Peter** (Luke 24. 33, 34; 1 Cor. 15. 5). This was in Jerusalem. What took place at this meeting has not been revealed.

5. **To ten disciples** (Luke 24. 36-43). Another account in John 20. 19-25. This was in the upper room in Jerusalem, where the Last Supper had been partaken, and it was on the evening of the day of resurrection.

6. **To eleven disciples** (John 20. 26-29). This was in the same place a week later.

7. **To seven disciples** at the Sea of Galilee (John 21. 1-22). At this interview Peter was reinstated in his apostleship.

8. **To five hundred disciples** (1 Cor. 15. 6). This was the official manifestation of Christ appointed before his death (Matt. 26. 32; 28. 16). It took place "on the mountain" (Rev. Ver.), probably where the Sermon on the Mount was preached. At this time the great commission was given (Matt. 28. 18-20).

9. **To James** (1 Cor. 15. 7). Nothing is known about this meeting. The relationship of James to Jesus (Mark 6. 3; Gal. 1. 19). Allusions to him in Acts 15. 13; 21. 18. His epistle (James 1. 1). Probably this appearance was in Jerusalem (Acts 1. 14).

10. **The Ascension** (Luke 24. 50-53; Acts 1. 9). This was at Bethany, on the eastern slope of the Mount of Olives (Acts 1. 12). The promise at his departure (Acts 1. 10, 11).

This list of appearances should be carefully memorized and the place of each noted on the map, with its circumstances and events.

IV. **The Traits of the Risen Christ.** There were some respects in which Jesus after his resurrection was the same as he had been before; but there were also some essential differences.

1. **He was the very same Jesus.** It was not a spirit, a disembodied ghost, which appeared to the disciples. He possessed personal identity, and was the living one whom the disciples had known before. See Luke 24. 39, 40; John 20. 27.

2. **He appeared only occasionally.** He did not come to remain with his people, for it was better for them that he should go away (John 16. 7). He manifested himself after his resurrection often enough to strengthen faith, but not enough to lead his disciples to lean upon his presence.

3. **He appeared to his disciples only** (Acts 10. 40, 41). Why he did not appear to unbelievers (Luke 16. 31). His personal ministry was ended, and henceforth he was to speak to men through his messengers (2 Cor. 5. 19, 20).

4. **He possessed a spiritual body.** There is a spiritual body (1 Cor. 15. 40-44). Christ possessed such a body, uncontrolled by physical law, but dominated by the spirit. He came and went at will (Luke 24. 36; John 20. 19). He withheld himself from recognition or permitted it as he chose (Luke 24. 15, 16; 24. 30, 31; John 20. 14-16; 21. 4-7). With us the body limits the spirit; with him the spirit controlled the body.

5. **He recognized individuals** after his resurrection. The grave had not blotted out his memory of the past nor of his personal regard for people. He called his friends by name after his resurrection (Matt. 28. 10; John 20. 16; 20. 26; 21. 15). He showed the same spirit of affection, of tenderness, and of patience with the mistakes of his followers as he had shown during his earthly life. His gentleness toward a sorrowing woman (John 20. 11-15). His kindness toward a doubting disciple (John 20. 24-29). His forgiveness of a denying disciple (John 21. 15-19). Such were the traits which he bore away from earth, and such are the traits which he bears still on his throne.

Blackboard Outline

The Forty Days of Resurrection

I. **Nec. Chr. Res.** 1. Nat. Ch. 2. Ful. pro. 3. Wo. red. 4. Fai. dis. 5. Att. Chr. auth. 6. Pl. ou. res.

II. **Fac. Chr. Res.** 1. Pro. tes. wit. 2. Eff. pow. G. 3. Fir. da. we. 4. Th. d. af. de.

III. **Ten. App. Je. af. Res.** 1. Ma. Mag. 2. Oth. wom. 3. Tw. dis. 4. Pet. 5. Ten dis. 6. Elev. dis. 7. Sev. dis. 8. Fiv. hun. dis. 9. Jas. 10. Asc.

IV. **Tra. Ris. Chr.** 1. Ver. sa. Jes. 2. Ap. on occ. 3. To dis. on. 4. Pos. spir. bod. 5. Rec. ind

Questions for Review

Why was the resurrection of Jesus Christ a necessity? What proves the fact of the resurrection? How was the resurrection effected? When did it take place? How long after the death of Jesus was his resurrection? How many times did Jesus appear after his resurrection? To whom did he appear first? What were the circumstances of this appearance? What were the five appearances on the day of resurrection? Name the instances when Jesus appeared during the forty days after the resurrection day. What were the traits of the risen Christ? What was the nature of his body after his resurrection?

ELEVENTH STUDY

The New Testament World

We have seen that the life of Jesus Christ while on earth was limited to the land of Palestine. But in a few years the church founded by his apostles overstepped the boundaries of that land; and its scope became world-wide. Therefore as we begin the history of the Early Church it becomes necessary for us to study **the New Testament World**.

Comparing the maps before us with that of the Old Testament World we find that in the four centuries between the events of the Old and New Testaments the dominion of the world passed from Asia to Europe, and Jerusalem, which had been in the center, became one of the cities upon the extreme east. Hence our map moves with the course of the empire westward a thousand miles.

I. We draw the outlines of the most important **Seas**. These are:

1. The **Mediterranean Sea**, from its eastern limits as far west as Italy. Voyages on it are referred to in Acts 9. 30; 13. 4; 21. 1, 2; 27. 3.

2. The **Sea of Galilee**, associated with the life of Christ. Find its three different names in Matt. 15. 29; John 6. 1; Luke 5. 1.

3. The **Dead Sea**, not named in the New Testament.

4. The **Black Sea**, north of Asia Minor.

5. The **Ægean Sea**, between Asia Minor and Greece. Voyages upon it (Acts 16. 11; 18. 18; 20. 13-15).

6. The **Adriatic Sea**, between Greece and Italy (Acts 27. 27).

II. In these seas are many **Islands**, of which we name five of the most noteworthy in New Testament history:

1. **Cyprus**, in the northeast corner of the Mediterranean (Acts 4. 36; 13. 4).

2. **Crete**, south of the Ægean Sea, between Asia Minor and Greece (Acts 27. 7; Titus 1. 5).

3. **Patmos**, in the Ægean Sea, not far from Ephesus (Rev. 1. 9).

4. **Sicily**, southwest of Italy (Acts 28. 12).

5. **Melita**, now Malta, south of Sicily (Acts 28. 1).

III. We locate the different **Provinces**, arranging them in four groups.

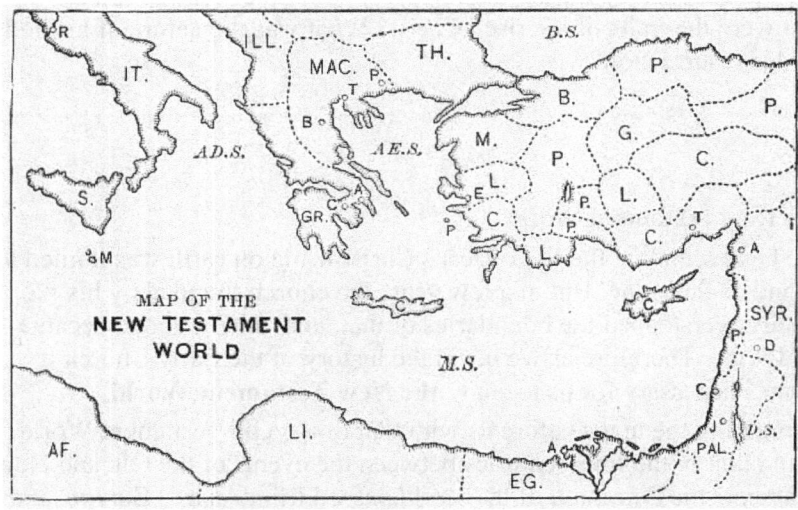

1. Those on the continent of **Europe** are: 1.) **Thrace.** 2.) **Macedonia** (Acts 14. 9, 10; 20. 1-3). 3.) **Greece**, also called **Achaia** (Acts 18. 12; 20. 3). 4.) **Illyricum** (Rom. 15. 19). 5.) **Italy** (Acts 27. 1).

2. Those on the continent of **Africa** are: 1.) **Africa Proper.** 2.) **Libya** (Acts 2. 10) 3.) **Egypt** (Matt. 2. 13).

3. Those on the continent of **Asia**, exclusive of Asia Minor, are: 1.) **Arabia**, perhaps referring to the desert region southeast of Palestine (Gal. 1. 17). 2.) **Judea**, the Jewish name for all Palestine, in the New Testament period (Luke 1. 5). 3.) **Phœnicia** (Mark 7. 24; Acts 15. 3; 21. 2). 4.) **Syria**, north of Palestine (Acts 15. 41; 20. 3).

4. The provinces in **Asia Minor** are so frequently mentioned in the Acts and Epistles that it is necessary for the student to learn their names and locations. We divide the fourteen provinces into four groups.

(*a*) Three on the Black Sea, beginning on the east. 1.) **Pontus** (Acts 18. 2). 2.) **Paphlagonia.** 3.) **Bithynia** (Peter 1. 1).

(*b*) Three on the Ægean Sea, beginning on the north. 4.) **Mysia** (Acts 16. 7). 5.) **Lydia.** 6.) **Caria.** These three provinces together formed the district known as "Asia" (Acts 2. 9; 19. 10).

(*c*) Three on the Mediterranean Sea, beginning on the west. 7.) **Lycia** (Acts 27. 5). 8.) **Pamphylia** (Acts 13. 13). 9.) **Cilicia** (Acts 21. 39).

(*d*) Five in the interior. 10.) On the north, **Galatia** (Gal. 1. 2). 11.) On the east, **Cappadocia** (Acts 2. 9). 12.) On the southeast, **Lycaonia** (Acts 14. 6). 13.) On the southwest, **Pisidia** (Acts 13. 14). 14.) On the west **Phrygia** (Acts 16. 6).

IV. We notice the twelve most important **Places**.

1. **Alexandria**, the commercial metropolis of Egypt (Acts 18. 24).

2. **Jerusalem**, the religious capital of the Jewish world (Matt. 4. 5; Luke 24. 47).

3. **Cæsarea**, the Roman capital of Judea (Acts 10. 1; 23. 23, 24).

4. **Damascus**, in the southern part of Syria (Acts 19. 3).

5. **Antioch**, the capital of Syria, in the north (Acts 11. 26; 13. 1).

6. **Tarsus**, the birthplace of St. Paul, in Cilicia (Acts 22. 3).

7. **Ephesus**, the metropolis of Asia Minor, in the province of Lydia (Acts 19. 1).

8. **Philippi**, in Macedonia, where the gospel was first preached in Europe (Acts 16. 12).

9. **Thessalonica**, the principal city in Macedonia (Acts 17. 1; Thess 1. 1).

10. **Athens**, the literary center of Greece (Acts 17. 16).

11. **Corinth**, the political capital of Greece (Acts 18. 1-12).

12. **Rome**, the imperial city (Acts 28. 16; Rom. 1. 7).

Other lands and places are referred to as Elam, Parthia, and Media, all east of the Euphrates river (Acts 2. 9). Ethiopia, south of Egypt in Africa (Acts 8. 27), and Babylon on the Euphrates (1 Peter 5. 13); but these places are outside the general history of the church.

Hints to the Teacher and Her Class. Eleventh Study

In teaching this lesson let the conductor sketch the outline of the map upon the board and drill upon the seas; then draw and name the islands; then drill upon the provinces, etc. Review until the lesson is learned by all the class.

The student should search all the references and be able to state the events connected with each locality.

It would be well for the student to find additional Scripture references to all the localities.

Let each student practice the drawing of the map at home, until he can draw it without copy. Then, in presence of the class, let one student draw on the blackboard in presence of the class the boundary lines of the continents; or one the boundary line in Asia; another in Europe; and a third in Africa. Then let another draw and name the islands; and others locate and name the provinces in Asia, Europe, and Africa; and finally let the twelve cities be located and named.

Blackboard Outline

I. Se. Med. Gal. De. Bl. Æg. Adr.

II. Isl. Cyp. Cre. Pat. Sic. Mel.

III **Prov.** 1. **Eur.** Thr. Mac. Gre. (Ach.) Ill. It. 2. **Afr.** Af.-Pr. Lib. Eg. 3. **Asi.** Ar. Jud. Phœ. Syr. 4. **As. Min.** (*a*) Pon. Paph. Bit. (*b*) Mys. Lyd. Car. (*c*) Lyc. Pam. Cil. (*d*) Gal. Cap. Lyc. Pi. Ph.

IV. **Pla.** Alex. Jer. Cæs. Dam. Ant. Tar. Eph. Phi. Thes. Ath. Cor. Ro.

Questions for Review

What difference is to be noted between the map of the Old Testament world and that of the New? Name six seas in the New Testament world. State the location of each of these seas. Name five islands in the New Testament world. Give the location of each island. Name in order the provinces in Europe in the New Testament world. Name the provinces in

Africa. Name the provinces in Asia, exclusive of Asia Minor. Name the provinces of Asia Minor bordering on the Black Sea. Name the provinces on the Ægean Sea. Name the provinces on the Mediterranean Sea. Name and locate each of the interior provinces. What city of the New Testament world was in Africa? What cities were in Judea and Syria? What cities were in Asia Minor? What cities were in Europe?

TWELFTH STUDY

The Synagogue

Before beginning the history of the Early Church, we must study one institution which formed an important link between the Old Testament and the New; and more than any other institution prepared the way for the gospel throughout the Jewish world. That institution was the synagogue.

I. **Its Origin.** The synagogue arose during the captivity, when the Temple was in ruins and the sacrifices were in abeyance. In the land of captivity the people of God met for worship and fellowship, and out of their meeting grew the synagogue, a word meaning "a coming together." It is believed that the institution was organized as a part of the Jewish system by Ezra, B. C. 440.

II. **Its Universality.** There was but one temple, standing on Mount Moriah, and only those who journeyed thither could attend its services. But the synagogue was in every place where the Jews dwelt, both in Palestine and throughout the world. Wherever ten Jewish heads of families could be found there a synagogue would be established. There were four hundred and sixty synagogues in Jerusalem; and every nationality of Jews had its own (Acts 6. 9).

III. **The Place of Meeting.** This might be a building erected for the purpose, or a hired room, or even a place in the open air (Acts 16. 13). This meeting place was employed for secular as well as religious uses. Courts were held in it, and sentence was administered (Acts 22. 19), and sometimes a school for teaching the law was held in it. Thus the synagogue became a center of local influence.

IV. **Its Arrangement.** Every ancient synagogue contained:

1. *An "ark,"* which was the chest for the sacred rolls, and stood in the end of the building toward Jerusalem.

2. *Chief seats*, elevated, near and around the "ark," for the elders and leading men (Matt. 23. 6).

3. A desk for the reader standing upon a platform.

4. Places for the worshipers, carefully graded according to rank, the Gentile visitors having seats near the door of entrance.

5. A lattice gallery where women could worship without being seen.

V. **Its Officers.** These were:

1. Three *rulers of the synagogue*, who directed the worship, managed the business details, and possessed a limited judicial authority over the Jews in the district (Mark 4. 22; Acts 13. 15). One of these was the presiding officer, and called "*the* ruler."

2. The *chazzan* (Luke 4. 20, "the minister"), who united the functions of clerk, schoolmaster, sexton, and constable to administer sentence on offenders.

3. The *batlanim*, "men of ease," seven men who were chosen to act as a legal congregation, were pledged to be present at the regular services, and sometimes received a small fee for being present.

VI. **Its Services.** These were held on Saturday, Monday, and Thursday, and were conducted by the members in turn, several taking part in each service. They consisted of:

1. Forms of prayer, conducted by a leader, with the responses by the worshipers.

2. Reading of selections from the law and the prophets, according to an appointed order (Acts 15. 21). The reading was in Hebrew, but it was translated, verse by verse, into the language of the people, whether Greek or Aramaic.

3. Exposition or comment upon the Scripture, in which any member might take part (Luke 4. 20, 21; Acts 13. 15, 16).

VII. **Its Influence.** It is easy to perceive how widely and how powerfully the results of such an institution would reach.

1. It perpetuated the worship of God and united the worshipers.

2. It supplied a more thoughtful and spiritual worship than the elaborate ritual of the Temple.

3. It promoted the study of the Old Testament Scriptures and made them thoroughly familiar to every Jew.

4. It attracted the devout and intelligent among the Gentiles, many of whom became worshipers of God and were known as "proselytes of the gate" (Acts 10. 1, 2).

VIII. **Its Preparation for the Gospel.** It is evident that the apostles and early Christian teachers were greatly aided by the synagogue.

1. It furnished a *place*; for everywhere the church began in the synagogue, even though it soon left it (Acts 13. 5; 18. 4; 19. 8).

2. It prepared a *people*; for the synagogue was attended by the earnest and thoughtful, both of Jews and Gentiles, who were thus made ready for the higher truths of the gospel (Acts 13. 42, 43).

3. It supplied a *plan of service*; for it is evident that the early Christian worship was modeled, not on the ritual of the Temple, but on the simpler forms of the synagogue.

4. It gave a *system of organization*; for the Government of the early church was similar to, and doubtless suggested by, that of the synagogue.

Blackboard Outline

I. **Ori.** Cap. Ez. B. C. 440.

II. **Univ.** 10 fam. 460 Jer.

III. **Pl. Meet.** Buil. ro. op. air. sec. us.

IV. **Arr.** 1. Ark. 2. Ch. sea. 3. Desk. 4. Pla. wor. 5. Gal.

V. **Off.** 1. Rul. 2. Chaz. 3. Batl.

VI. **Serv.** 1. Pr. 2. Reac. Ser. 3. Exp.

VII. **Inf.** 1. Per. wor. 2. Spir. wor. 3. St. O. T. 4. Attr. Gen.

VIII. **Prep. Gosp.** 1. Pla. 2. Peo. 3. Ser. 4. Org.

Review Questions

Between what two institutions was the synagogue a link of connection? How did the synagogue originate? Who gave it definite organization? Wherein did it differ from the temple and its services? Where were synagogues formed? How many were in Jerusalem? What buildings and places were used for the synagogue service? To what secular uses were these buildings put? What were the arrangements of the synagogue? Where did the women worship? What was "the ark" in the synagogue? Who were the officers? What was the *chazzan*? Who were the *batlanim*? What were the services of the synagogue? What influence did the synagogue exert? Whom did the synagogue benefit outside of the Jews? How did the synagogue prepare the way for the gospel?

THIRTEENTH STUDY
The Church in Judea

Part One

From the Ascension of Christ A. D. 30, to the Appointment of the Seven A. D. 35.

We now enter upon the second great subject in New Testament history, the Early Church. This will include the annals of the church from the Ascension of Christ, A. D. 30, to the end of the apostolic age, A. D. 100. This epoch of seventy years is divided into four periods:

1. *The church in Judea*, from the Ascension of Christ, A. D. 30, to the Appointment of the Seven, A. D. 35.

2. *The church in Transition*, from the Appointment of the Seven, A. D. 35, to the Council at Jerusalem, A. D. 50.

3. *The church among the Gentiles*, from the Council at Jerusalem, A. D. 50, to the death of St. Paul, A. D. 68.

4. *The End of the Age*, from the death of St. Paul to the death of St. John, about A. D. 100. It should be noted that all of these dates are uncertain and historians are not agreed with reference to them.

Of these four periods we take up the first, the church in Judea, or "The church of the First Days;" a space of about five years. During this time the work of the church was confined wholly to the Jewish people, and apparently to the immediate region of Jerusalem.

I. We notice the **Events of this Period**.

1. **The followers of Christ** immediately after the Ascension; a company of people believing in Jesus as the Messiah of Israel.

1.) *Their number* was 120 (Acts 1. 15). They were mostly from Galilee (Acts 2. 7). They were all the organized church at that time, although throughout the land were thousands more ready to unite with them.

2.) *Their meeting place* was "the upper room" (Acts 1. 13), on Mount Zion, probably the room where the "Last Supper" was held. Some think that this may have been the house of Mary the mother of Mark, referred to in Acts 12. 1, 2.

3.) *Their religious condition* between the Ascension and Pentecost was probably that of belief in Jesus as the King of Israel, but with the conception of an earthly kingdom (Acts 1. 6). They were waiting with prayer for divine direction (Acts 1. 14).

2. **The Outpouring of the Spirit** came upon this company on the day of Pentecost, ten days after the Ascension, fifty days after the Crucifixion. The spirit descended upon them all in the form of "tongues of fire."

1.) *Physical effect.* This was "the gift of tongues," a mysterious influence (Acts 2. 2, 3). This was not a power to speak foreign languages at will; but probably a strange divine speech, sounding to everyone who heard it as though it were the language of his own people (Acts 2. 8).

2.) *Mental effect.* There came to these disciples a revelation, once and for all, of Christ's kingdom. not as a political state, but as a spiritual institution; a society of believers of which Jesus in glory is the invisible yet real head.

3.) *Spiritual effect.* This was the personal presence of the Holy Spirit with each member; an indwelling life given not merely to the apostles, but to each and every disciple; a divine enthusiasm, giving guidance, enlightenment, power. Nor was that divine life limited to that company. It has dwelt ever since in the church of Christ, and in each member of the church, (1 Cor. 3. 16; 6. 19).

3. **The Testimony of the Gospel.** 1.) The first effect of this new endowment of the Holy Spirit was a strong testimony to the gospel of Christ; a proclamation of *Jesus as the Messiah King*; and this testimony was the conquering weapon of the church. 2.) This testimony was given by *all* the members. It is a mistake to suppose that the church settled down in Jerusalem with Peter as its pastor and preacher. Peter was the leader, but not the ruler of the church. Find four addresses of Peter sketched in Acts 2-5; not "sermons" after the modern method, but ardent declarations of Jesus as the Messiah; and similar testimonies were given by all the members everywhere, in synagogues, in houses, publicly and privately.

4. **The Apostolic Miracles.** 1.) At the opening of the history of the church we read of a *number of miracles*. a) A lame man healed. (Acts 3. 1-10). b) A miracle of judgment (Acts 5. 1-10). c) More miracles of healing (Acts 5. 12-16). 2.) We can see the *purpose of these* miracles and how they were needed by the church in the day of its weakness. (a) They attracted *attention* to the gospel. (b) They gave *authority* to the apostles as teachers. (c) They were *illustrations* of the spiritual work of the gospel; i. e., healing of the lame man a type of salvation.

5. **The Persecution of the Apostles.** It was inevitable that the preaching of the apostles and the growing prominence of the church should arouse opposition from the men who a few months before had crucified Jesus. A persecution was begun, at first upon Peter and John,

then upon all the apostles. It was not sharp, murderous, crushing out the church. The apostles were first threatened (Acts 4. 17), then imprisoned (Acts 5. 18), then scourged (Acts 5. 40). The persecution only attracted greater notice to the gospel, and led to increasing numbers of believers.

6. **The Growth of the Church** went on through all these experiences. Beginning with 120, on the day of Pentecost 3,000 were received by baptism (Acts 2. 41). There was a daily growth after (Acts 2. 47). Soon the number grew to 5,000, besides women and children (Acts 4. 4). Another increase is named in Acts 5. 14; also again in Acts 6. 7.

7. The last event in this period was **the Appointment of the Seven**. Read the account in Acts 6. 1-7. Notice for the first time in this history a reference to the two great classes of Jews. 1.) *Hebrews*, Jews whose ancestors had lived in Palestine, and who spoke the Hebrew tongue, though with Syriac admixture. 2.) *Grecian Jews* (frequently called Hellenists). Jews descended from exiles who had remained abroad in foreign lands, otherwise "Jews of the Dispersion." Everywhere except in Palestine these foreign Jews were far more numerous than the Hebrews, and they were also the richer and more intelligent. They spoke the Greek language.

Note also that the seven men named in this account are nowhere spoken of as "deacons." From Acts 21. 8 we learn that they were called "the seven." They were not an order in the church, but a committee appointed for a service.

Blackboard Outline

Per. 1. Ch. Jud. 2. Ch. Trans. 3. Ch. am. Gen. 4. E. A.

Ch.

1. **in Jud.** 1. **Ev. Per.**

2. **Foll. Ch.** 1.) Num. 2.) Meet-pl. 3.) Rel. Con.

3. **Out Sp.** 1.) Phys. eff. 2.) Men. eff. 3.) Spir. eff.

4. **Tes. Gosp.** 1.) Jes. Mess. K. 2.) By all.

5. **Ap. Mir.** 1.) Num. mir. 2.) Pur. Att. Auth. Illus.

Per. Ap.

6. **Gro. Ch.** 120, 3,000, 5,000. "Multitude."

7. **App. Sev.** Heb. Gre. (Hellen.)

Review Questions. Part One

How long a period is embraced in the history of the New Testament church? Name four periods in the history, and the events with which each begins and ends. How long a time is embraced in the first period? By what name is the first period called? State in order the seven events in the first period. What was the number of Christ's followers in Jerusalem immediately after his Ascension? Where did they meet? What was their religious condition? What took place ten days after the Ascension of Christ? On what day did this outpouring occur? What were the physical effects of this outpouring? What were the mental effects? What were the spiritual effects? What testimony was given by the apostles and church? How many addresses of Peter at this time are mentioned? What miracles were wrought? How did these miracles benefit the church? What persecution arose? What was the nature of this persecution? Against whom was it directed? Did it harm the church? What is said of the growth of the church during this epoch? Who were "the seven"? How were they chosen? For what were they appointed? What two classes of Jesus are named? Define each class.

Part Two

II. Having studied the history we now look at the **General Aspects of the Pentecostal Church**.

1. **Its locality**: entirely in Judea, and apparently in and around Jerusalem. There is no mention during this early period of churches in Galilee, although most of the earliest members were Galileans (Acts 1. 11; 2. 7). Individual believers doubtless were to be found throughout the land, but outside of Jerusalem they were not yet gathered together in assemblies and not yet endowed with the Spirit.

2. **Its membership** was composed wholly of Jews. As yet not a single Gentile had been received, and apparently there was no thought of Gentile believers. Christianity began as a Jewish society. Three classes of Jews were embraced in its membership: 1.) *Hebrews*, or Palestinian Jews. 2.) *Grecians* or Hellenists, Jews of the Dispersion. 3.) *Proselytes*, or Gentiles who had embraced Judaism and received circumcision (Acts 6. 5).

3. **The qualifications for membership** were: 1.) *Repentance*, which meant not so much sorrow as decision for Christ. 2.) *Faith in Jesus* as Christ; i. e., submission to Jesus as the true King of Israel. 3.) *Baptism* in the name of Jesus the Christ as the outward form of consecration.

4. **The spirit of the Pentecostal Church.** 1.) In theory, and for the most part in fact, every member *possessed the Holy Spirit*, an abounding, directing spiritual life. Every member was conscious of the immediate presence of God, and lived in this fellowship. 2.) This inspired a *Christian fellowship*, the love of the brotherhood. 3.) As a result of this divine and human fellowship came *liberal giving* to each other's needs. There was a voluntary and limited "community of goods," the rich giving freely to aid the poor; which led to some insincere imitation. See the contrast of Barnabas and Ananias (Acts 4. 34-37; 5. 1-11).

5. **Doctrines.** The doctrinal aspects of Christianity at that early period were less prominent than its spirit. As yet there was no such theological system as arose later. Three great doctrines were held fervently: 1.) *The resurrection of Jesus*; that he had risen and was living. 2.) *The Messiahship of Jesus*; that he was the prince of the true spiritual kingdom of Israel. 3.) *The return of Jesus as Christ*; that he would soon come again to earth.

6. **Worship and institutions.** These were: 1.) *The temple worship* attended by the disciples of Christ as by all worshiping Jews (Acts 2. 46; 3. 1). 2.) *The synagogue services*, twice each week; held everywhere throughout the city; with Scripture reading, prayer and testimony. 3.) "*The upper room*" was for a time the headquarters of the church; but Solomon's porch in the temple soon took its place (Acts 5. 12). 4.) "Breaking bread," which was the Holy Communion or the Lord's Supper; at that time observed not in public assemblies but as a family ordinance, at home (Acts 2. 42, 46). 5.) *The baptism* of new members.

7. **Government.** Scarcely any government or discipline was needed in a church where the Spirit of God was recognized as dwelling in each member. The apostles were revered as leaders, but were not exactly rulers over the body of believers. "The Seven" (Acts 6. 3) were not officials or "deacons," but laymen charged with specific duties.

8. **Literature.** 1.) *The Old Testament*; familiar to all, read in the synagogue, was seen now in a new light and with new meaning. 2.) *The teachings of Jesus*, as yet unwritten, were in the memory of most of the members who had heard his words; and especially in the memory of the apostles; but no books of the New Testament were by this time in writing.

9. **Leaders of the church.** 1.) Throughout this period *Peter* stands at the front as the ruling spirit of the church, by his endowments of mind, and especially by his promptness in word and act. 2.) With him stands *John* (Acts 3. 1; 4. 19). 3.) *Barnabas* won notice by his liberality and gifts of preaching (Acts 4. 36, 37). His name means "the speaker" or "the preacher." 4.) At the end of the period *Stephen* comes into notice.

Blackboard Outline

I. **Gen. Asp. Pen. Ch.**

1. **Loc.** Jud. Jer.

2. **Mem.** Jews. 1.) Heb. 2.) Gre. Hel. 3.) Pros.

3. **Qual. Mem.** 1.) Rep. 2.) Fai. 3.) Bap.

4. **Spir.** 1.) Poss. H. S. 2.) Chr. fell. 3.) Lib. giv.

5. **Doc.** 1.) Res. Jes. 2.) Mess. Jes. 3.) Ret. Jes.

6. **Worsh. and Inst.** 1.) Tem. 2.) Syn. 3.) "Up. ro" 4.) "Bre. br." 5.) Bap.

7. **Gov.** Sp. Apos. Sev.

8. **Lit.** 1.) O. T. 2.) Tea. Jes.

9. **Lead.** 1.) Pet. 2.) Jo. 3.) Bar. 4.) Ste.

Review Questions. Part Two

Where was the church located during the Pentecostal period? Were there churches or members in Galilee? To what race did all the members belong? What were the three classes in its membership? Who were Hebrews? Who were Grecians? By what other name were they called? Who were the "proselytes"? What were the requisites for membership in the church? What is said of the spirit of this church? How did this spirit lead the members to regard each other? What is said of their gifts to each other? Were doctrines made prominent in the church? What three doctrines were held by the members? What institutions of worship were maintained? What other institutions were observed? What is meant by "breaking bread"? Where was this service held? What is said as to the government of the church? What was the position of the apostles? What were "the seven"? What literature did the church possess at this time? What knowledge did they have of the teachings of Jesus? Who were the leaders of the church in this period?

FOURTEENTH STUDY
The Church in Transition
From the Appointment of the Seven, A. D. 35, to the Council at Jerusalem, A. D. 50.

We enter upon the study of a brief period, only fifteen years, but of supreme importance and of vast results to the world; a period, too, in which we have the deepest interest, for if its events had never taken place Christianity would have been only a Jewish sect and we would not be members of it.

1. At its opening, 35 A. D., the church was in and around Jerusalem only; and every member was a Jew, bound by the restrictions of the Jewish law and ceremony. There was no thought that the church would ever include Gentiles except as Gentiles might first become proselytes to Judaism.

2. At its close, 50 A. D., we see a church planted all around the northeastern portion of the Mediterranean Sea; and, what is even more remarkable, a church wherein Jews and Gentiles were worshiping together on terms of equality. A wonderful transition this!

I. Let us draw **the Map of the Lands** occupied by the church during those fifteen years. 1. Draw the coast line of the Mediterranean Sea. 2. The island of Cyprus. 3. The lands east of the Mediterranean Sea. Judea (or Palestine), Syria, Phœnicia. 4. The lands north of the Mediterranean Sea, in Asia Minor, Cilicia, Pamphylia, Pisidia, Lycaonia. 5. The places: Jerusalem, Joppa, Cæsarea and Samaria in Judea, Damascus and Antioch in Syria, Tarsus in Cilicia, Antioch in Pisidia, Lystra and Derbe in Lycaonia.

II. Let us carefully note the **Progress of Events** in this remarkable evolution of the church.

1. **The Preaching of Stephen.** Stephen was a Hellenist, or a Jew of foreign origin. He was the man who first had the vision of a church wider than the bounds of Judaism; and he proclaimed this great truth. See evidences of this in:

1.) The new and bitter *enmity* which his teaching aroused (Acts 6. 12).

2.) The *accusation* against him, which contained a half truth (Acts 6. 11, 13, 14).

3.) The *prominence* of the man, and his discourse, the longest public discourse reported in the New Testament, except the Sermon on the Mount (Acts 7. 1-53).

4.) The *logical aim* of his address: to show that the Jews had shown themselves unworthy of their trust, implying that it would be given to others. This sermon was never finished, being broken up by the riotous acts of the council.

2. **Saul's Persecution** (Acts 8. 1-3). We shall study this man's early history later. (See page 96). He was intense and furious in his loyalty to Judaism, and undertook to crush out the gospel of Christ by violent measures. See Acts 22. 4; 26. 10, 11; Gal. 1. 13. 1.) As a result the Pentecostal church was broken up and its members were scattered. 2.) But, as another effect, these disciples who were scattered went everywhere preaching (Acts 8. 4). These "preachers" were not the apostles; they were lay-members; not delivering sermons, but testifying in country synagogues and in homes the gospel of Christ. 3.) Another result followed, churches sprang up throughout Judea (Acts 9. 31), Samaria (Acts 8. 14), and Syria (Acts 9. 2, 10; Acts 11. 19). Thus Saul by his persecution unconsciously aided the spread of the gospel.

3. **The Gospel in Samaria** (Acts 8. 5-8). One of these disciples, Philip (not the apostle, but one of the "seven" Acts 6. 5), went to Samaria, and there preached with great success. A significant event, showing breadth of view and victory over prejudice. See John 4. 9. The Samaritans were regarded, not exactly as Gentiles, but as irregular and inferior, and despised even more than Gentiles. Still more significant, the Samaritan church was recognized by the apostles and received the gift of the Holy Spirit (Acts 8. 14-17). Note also that, after his work in Samaria, Philip went down to the coast and established a chain of churches from Azotus to Cæsarea (Acts 8. 40).

4. **Peter's Vision** (Acts 10. 1-48), and the events accompanying it, was the next step in the forward movement of the church. The leading apostle and most prominent man in the church, under direction of the Spirit, journeys thirty miles to preach to a little company of Gentiles; the Spirit falls upon them, another Pentecost; and Peter baptizes them. Here, then, is a genuine church of Gentiles founded by an apostle; the first fruits of a great harvest.

5. The next step is even more momentous in its results, **the Conversion of Saul** (Acts 9. 1-19). It seems to be a sudden conversion, but one

expression (Acts 9. 5) shows that Saul had been struggling against conviction. His enmity had not been so greatly against "Jesus as Christ" as against "Christ for all the world" i. e., the gospel as preached by Stephen; and when converted he went fully over to Stephen's view, and became Stephen's successor, with even larger vision. Note the order of events in Saul's early ministry. 1.) Preaching in Damascus (Acts 9. 20-22). 2.) Retirement to Arabia (Gal. 1. 17). This may mean almost anywhere to the east or south of Palestine. In our opinion, he went thither not to meditate nor to study theology, but to preach in the cities between Palestine and the desert. 3.) Again preaching in Damascus (Gal. 1. 17). His escape (Acts 9. 23-25). 4.) Visit to Jerusalem (Acts 9. 26-28). Whom he met on this visit (Gal. 1. 8, 19). The event which led to his departure from Jerusalem (Acts 22. 17-21). 5.) His return to his birthplace (Acts 9. 29, 30. Gal. 1. 21). Let the student draw on the map all the journeys of Saul, beginning with his journey from Jerusalem to Damascus before his conversion.

VI. **The Church at Antioch.** (Acts 11. 19-30). Antioch was the third city of the Roman empire; capital of Syria, of which Judea was a dependency. Its many Jews had their synagogues, each with its "court of the Gentiles," where the Gentile worshipers sat during the services. In the story of this church note 1.) Its unnamed founders (Acts 11. 19). 2.) Its membership of both Jews and Gentiles (Acts 11. 20). See American Revised Version. 3.) Its prominence (Acts 11. 22-26). 4.) Its liberality (Acts 11. 27-30). 5.) Some of its workers (Acts 13. 1). 6.) Note how Saul came to be associated with this church (Acts 11. 25, 26).

VII. **The First Missionary Journey** (Acts 13. 1-4). Another step in advance was taken when two missionaries went out to plant churches of both Jews and Gentiles. 1.) They were called by the Holy Spirit (ver. 2). 2.) Approved by the church (Ver. 3). 3.) Their method; whenever possible beginning with the synagogue, where they would have access both to devout Jews and devout Gentiles (Acts 13. 5). 4.) The lands visited. Cyprus (Acts 13. 4-6). Pisidia (Acts 13. 14). Lycaonia (Acts 14. 6). On the return journey, Pamphylia (Acts 14. 24, 25). Let the student draw the maps showing the lands and places, and the route of the journey. One province in the southern tier was left unvisited, Cilicia, because Paul had already preached there (Gal. 1. 21-23).

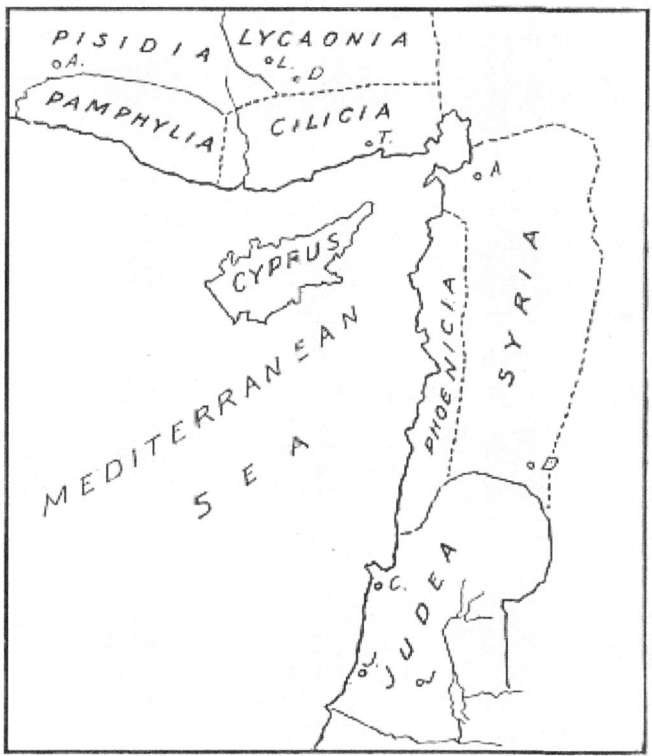

VIII. **The Council at Jerusalem** (Acts 15). Of course such a spread of the gospel among the Gentiles would be very unwelcome to narrow Jewish believers. Their complaint and demand (Acts 15. 1, 2). Who attended the Council at Jerusalem (Acts 15. 2-4). Who took prominent part in it (Acts 15. 7, 13). The conclusion of the Council (Acts 15. 27-29).

The great question was now settled. Jews and Gentiles were standing at last on equality in the church, and the great transition from a Jewish church to a church for all the world was accomplished.

Hints to the Teacher and the Student

1. Read carefully in the book of Acts from the 8th to the 15th chapter, inclusive.

2. Draw the map first from copy, then without copy; not seeking for accuracy, but aiming rather for correct relation of the lands to each other.

3. Study each section of the lesson; look up every reference, and note its relation to the general subject. Master the eight points in the outline thoroughly.

4. Draw on the map (or, better, on a series of maps) the following journeys: 1.) Philip's journeys. Acts 8. 2.) Peter's journeys. Acts 8 and 10. 3.) Saul's early journeys. 4.) The journey of Saul and Barnabas. 5.) The journeys in connection with the council at Jerusalem, going and returning.

5. Let the teacher call upon the scholars to tell as a story each of the eight points in the lesson, not from the text-book but from the book of Acts; each story by a student in turn.

Blackboard Outline

Ch. in Trans. 1.) Op. 2.) Clo.

I **Map.** Lands. Cy. Ju. Syr. Ph. Cil. Pam. Pi. Lyc. Places. Jer. Jop. Cæs. . Dam. Ant. Tar. An (Pi) Lys. Der.

I.
Prog. of Ev. 1. **Pre. Ste.** 1.) En. 2.) Acc. 3.) Prom. 4.) Log. ai.

2. **Sau. Per.** Res. 1.) Pen. Ch. bro. up. 2.) Dis. everyw. prea. 3.) Chur. spr. up.

3. **Gosp. in Sam.** Phil.

4. **Pet. Vis.** Pet. and Corn.

5. **Conv. Sau.** Sau. ear. Min. 1.) Dam. 2.) Ara. 3.) Dam. 4.) Jeru. 5.) Tar.

6. **Ch. at. Ant.** 1.) Foun. 2.) Mem. 3.) Prom. 4.) Lib. 5.) Work. 6.) Sau. asso.

7. **Fir. Miss. Jour.** 1.) Cal. 2.) App. 3.) Meth. 4.) Lands. C. P. L. P.

8. **Coun. at Jer.**

Review Questions

With what events did the period of transition begin and end? How long was it? What was the state of the church when it opened? What was the state of the church when it closed? Name an island and seven lands connected with this period. Name ten places connected with the period. State the eight great events in the history of the church at this time. What preacher introduced this epoch? How do we know that he preached salvation for the Gentiles? What man's persecution at this time proved a help to the church? Tell the story of this persecution. What three results followed it? Who formed the church in Samaria? Who were the Samaritans? How was the church recognized? Tell the story of a remarkable vision on a housetop. To what did that vision lead? Tell the story of a persecutor's conversion to Christ. Where did this conversion take place? What were the events in Saul's life that followed this conversion? What important church arose in Syria? Who were its founders? Who constituted its membership? Who were its leaders? What facts showed its prominence and influence? How came Saul to be associated with this church? Who went out as missionaries? Who went with them as helper? What became of this young man? What was their method of work? What lands did they visit? In what cities did they found churches? What led to the council at Jerusalem? Who attended the council? Who spoke in it? What were its conclusions? How did this end the period of transition in the church?

FIFTEENTH STUDY
The Church Twenty Years After the Ascension

We have now studied the two earliest periods in the history of the Christian church and have come to the year 50 A. D., twenty years after the Ascension of Christ and the outpouring of the Spirit on the first Pentecost. Let us look over the field and see what at that time was the state of the church.

I. **Its Extent.** Let the student draw again the map given with the last lesson, and locate upon it the following **lands**: 1. Judea (Palestine). 2. Syria. 3. Phœnicia. 4. Cyprus. 5. Cilicia. 6. Pamphylia. 7. Pisidia. 8. Lycaonia. In all these lands churches were established and at work.

II. **Its Membership.** The members of the church consisted of two classes of people, widely apart by nature, but brought together by the gospel:

1. There were churches where all the members were **Jews**, as in Judea. These were all faithful to the regulations of the Jewish ceremonial law, and many of them almost bigoted in their opinions concerning it (Acts 15. 1, 5).

2. There were other churches, as in Lycaonia, where all or nearly all the members were **Gentiles** (Acts 14. 6-13). In these the Jewish rules were unrecognized, almost unknown.

3. Between these two extremes was the great body of churches of **both Jews and Gentiles**. The two classes worshiped together; Jews remaining Jews, and Gentiles remaining Gentiles; but probably received the Lord's Supper apart, as it was as yet a house-service, not held at the public meetings.

4. While in most churches there was harmony, on both sides there were some radical members; but especially among the Jews. These were the

Judaizers; men who sought to compel all the disciples to receive circumcision, obey the ceremonial law and make the Christian church subordinate to Jewish ritualism. These were the enemies of Paul to the end of his ministry, perverting the Gentile churches and opposing the apostle's work.

III. **Its Leaders.** Three names stand out prominently at this time: 1. **Paul**, as the leader of the church in its world-wide plans, the apostle to the Gentiles (Gal. 2. 7). 2. **James**, as leader of the Jewish but not Judaizing elements (Acts 13. 13, 19). This was not James the apostle, for he had been put to death some time before this (Acts 12. 2); but James "the brother of the Lord" (Gal. 1. 19). He was the head of the church in Jerusalem and author of the Epistle of James. 3. **Peter**, who stood in friendly relation to both parties in the church, although his conduct was not always perfectly consistent with regard to Jewish regulations (Acts 11. 2, 3; Gal. 2. 11-14). Between these three leaders there was a clear understanding and no strong division of spirit, although they might not agree in all points. 4. Other leaders in this period were **Philip** (Acts 8. 40; 21. 8). **Barnabas**, **Silas** of Jerusalem and Antioch (Acts 15. 22, 32, 40), and **Titus** (Gal. 2. 1-4).

IV. **Its Government.** In our time the church is often a highly wrought organization, with articles of faith, orders, and officials of various grades. We are apt to assume such a condition in the early church. But at the time of which we speak there was very little organization or machinery; and there was little need of any, for a special reason: *Every member was under the direct guidance of the Holy Spirit*, living in fellowship with God, without mediation of priest or church. Yet we find certain officers named in the church:

1. **Apostles**, originally "the twelve," but changes arose and others were called by the title, for example, Paul and Barnabas (Acts 14. 14); James (Gal. 1. 19). The work of the apostles was not primarily government, but inspired testimony to Jesus as the Christ (Acts 1. 22; 6. 4); nowhere in Acts are the apostles represented as ruling the church (Acts 15. 6, 22).

2. **Elders** (Acts 11. 30; 14. 23; 15. 4). These were analogous to the same officers in the synagogue, from which the plan of the local churches was taken.

3. **Prophets** (Acts 11. 27, 28; Acts 13. 1; Acts 15. 32). Men who spoke out of direct fellowship with the Lord, and under inspiration of the Spirit; sometimes, though not always, giving predictions of future events.

4. **Teachers** (Acts 13. 1). Men who gave instruction in the Christian character; probably largely from recollection or knowledge of the

teaching of Christ. The difference between "prophesy" and "teaching" was that the former was the more spontaneous and the latter the more educative in the principles of the gospel.

V. **Its Doctrinal Views.** These remained substantially as in the first period. There was little tendency toward intellectual questionings while the church remained under Jewish influence. The discussion was rather regarding Jewish ceremonial regulations. The Messiahship, Resurrection and Return of Jesus were still the prominent teaching of the period.

VI. **Its Moral Standards.** The church is now face to face with the heathen world and all its abominable vices. Heathen moralists continually made excuse for the immorality which was so generally practiced. But Christianity made no compromise; set forth the high standard of the gospel, with the character of Christ as its ideal. This high standard unswervingly maintained was one secret of the church's power and growth. Notice, a little later than this period, in St. Paul's writings, the strong ethical spirit.

VII. **Its Meeting-places.** As yet "churches" or buildings for worship were not erected. The disciples met with the Jews in the synagogue or established synagogues of their own (James 2. 2). Often they met, even later than this period, in the upper rooms of private houses (Acts 20. 8; Rom. 16. 3-5; Philem. 2).

VIII. **Its Literature.** This was still the **Old Testament** only; no book of the New Testament having been written as early as 50 A. D. These writings were familiar to all the Jewish members, and almost equally familiar to the Gentiles who attended the synagogue. Was there an "oral gospel" in existence? Probably not in any set, authorized form; but repeated as the narration of teachings and works of Jesus. The tendency would naturally be for these teachings to settle into a few accepted forms or "gospels."

IX. Wherein did **the Unity of the Church** consist? Not in organization, nor government, nor doctrinal statement; but in a **common spiritual life**. They were of one heart and one mind, loved each other, contributed to each other's needs (Acts 11. 29; Gal. 2. 10), visited each other's churches (Acts 11. 22, 27, 30; 13. 25; 15. 27, 32). This was, and is, true church unity.

Blackboard Outline
Ch. 20 Ye. af. Asc.
I. **Ext.** Ja. Sy. Ph. Cy. Cil. Pam. Pi. Lyc.

II. **Mem.** 1. Je. 2. Gen. 3. Both J. and G. 4. "Judai."
III. **Lead.** 1. Pau. 2. Jam. 3. Pet. 4. Phi. 5. Bar. 6. Sil. 7. Tit.
IV. **Gov.** (Dir. Guid. H. S). 1. Aps. 2. El. 3. Pro. 4. Tea.
V. **Doc. Vie.** Mes. Res. Ret. Jes.
VI. **Mor. Stan.** "No comp."
VII. **Meet. Pla.** Syn. "Up. roo."
VIII. **Lit.** O. T. "Or. gosp."
IX. **Uni.** Com. spir. lif.

Review Questions

What stage in the church's progress do we now consider? In what lands was the church established at this time? What two classes of people constituted its membership? How did these two classes worship together? What service was observed in the homes of members? Who were the Judaizers? What harm did they do? Name the three great leaders at this time. Who was James? Give an instance when Peter was not entirely consistent in his conduct. Name four other leaders and a fact about each. Why did the church of that time need very little government? Name four kinds of officers in the church. What was the special work of the apostles? Where did the elders originate? With what churches are elders named in this period? What were the prophets in the church? Name some who are called prophets in this period. What was the work of teachers in the church? Were doctrinal studies or discussions prominent at this time? What were the three prominent doctrines of the church? Why do the moral standards of the church come into prominence at this time? What were those standards? Where did the Christians hold their meetings? What was the literature of the church at this time? What do you understand by "the oral gospel?" Was such a gospel in existence? Wherein did the unity of the church consist? How was this unity shown?

SIXTEENTH STUDY

The Preparation of Paul for his Work

Part One

Before we enter upon the study of "The church among the Gentiles," our next period, there is a preliminary topic to be considered. The only record which we possess of the period before us, the Book of Acts, not only represents Paul as the leading worker for the gospel, but it even omits all reports of the work of other apostles and evangelists. There must have been other workers: Peter, Barnabas, Philip, and other workers were still living, and must have been active in founding churches; but their work is not mentioned. We find mention of churches which Paul had not founded (Acts 21. 3, 7; Acts 28. 13, 14, 15). Paul stands before us as the leading and the typical worker in the gospel. We will therefore take for our theme, **The Preparation and Methods of Paul**.

At A. D. 50 Paul is now at Antioch, about fifty years old, having been born probably about four years after Jesus Christ. His first missionary journey has taken place, and he is now about to enter upon his second missionary journey. Let us notice some of his advantages for leadership in the gospel.

I. He was **a Jew**. (See Phil. 3. 5; Rom. 11. 1). The leader in this movement must be a Jew. 1. Because as a Jew he would have a *training* in Bible knowledge, and in the *faith* of a coming Messiah such as no Gentile could possess. 2. Moreover the work in nearly all places must begin in the synagogue. (See Acts 17. 1; 2. 10; 18. 1, 4; 19. 1, 8). And only a Jew could take part in its services.

II. He was a **Trained and Recognized Rabbi**: an accredited teacher of the law; "a college man" with the prestige of scholarship won in the school of Gamaliel, the greatest Jewish master of that age (Acts 5. 34; Acts 22. 3). Such a teacher would be welcome in any synagogue. In this respect contrast Paul with Peter and the other apostles (Acts 4. 13).

III. He was a **Hellenist**, or "Grecian Jew;" i. e., a Jew of the Dispersion; by birth and environment broader than the Jews of Jerusalem, who rarely came in contact with Gentiles. He was a traveler acquainted with the world; spoke Greek as fluently as Hebrew, an absolute necessity for preaching to Gentiles (Acts 21. 37, 40). He spoke to the Greek philosophers in their own tongue and after their own manner. Contrast Acts 17. 22 with Acts 22. 1. Tradition says that Peter, when at Rome, used an interpreter in preaching to the church. Paul's ability to speak at least two languages gave him a great advantage.

IV. Another advantage was that he was by birth a **Roman Citizen** (Acts 16. 37. Acts 22. 25-28). This privilege, at that time rare among those outside of Italy, gave the apostle safety, immunity from imprisonment by the local rulers, and the right to a trial before a Roman judge, with appeal to the emperor. James was put to death, and Peter thrown into prison by King Herod (Acts 12. 2-4); but Paul was by his citizenship undoubtedly saved more than once from torture and from death.

V. He was a divinely-called **Apostle**. When he spoke it was with all the fervor and authority of one who had seen the Lord and had received a special command from the lips of the ascended Christ to bear testimony to his gospel. His call came with his conversion (Acts 26. 12-19). He claimed the authority of an apostle (Gal. 1. 1; 1 Cor. 9. 1). Notice that in his letters Paul always places "apostles" before "prophets" (Eph. 2. 20; 3. 5; 4. 11), as holding the higher office in the church.

VI. He possessed rare **Natural Endowments** for his work.

1. He was a man of *sympathy*, warm-hearted and tender; making strong friendships, drawing men after him. Note how in every place he found friends (Acts 19. 31; 20. 4; 27. 3, 43).

2. He was a *preacher* of power. He was a master of the art of public speaking; and people would always listen to him with the deepest interest (Acts 17. 22-31. Acts 22. 1-2. Acts 26. 1-26).

3. He was a *theologian*. He saw the great truths of the gospel in clearer light than any of his co-workers. Under the guidance of the Spirit he formulated a system of doctrine (Gal. 1. 11, 12), which he sometimes called "my gospel" (Rom. 2. 16; 2 Tim. 2. 8). This "gospel according to Paul," presented in his great epistles, came to be the theology of the church, and so remains.

4. He possessed rare *tact* in dealing with men; knew how to adapt his methods to people of varied races and views. His manner of preaching at Athens was very different from that in Jerusalem. Note 1 Cor. 9. 19-22.

5. He was a *natural leader* of men; ready to take responsibilities, quick to decide, yet thoughtful of others. He possessed the ruling spirit, yet was no imperious, self-willed man. People were as ready to follow as he was to lead.

6. He was a *tireless worker*; indomitable and undiscouraged, caring little for hardship (2 Cor. 11. 23-28), although he seems to have been delicate in health. See allusions 2 Cor. 12. 7-10. Gal. 4. 13. Notice the field of his labors, in the middle of his ministry (Rom. 15. 19). Notice too his plans for regions more distant (Rom. 15. 24).

Blackboard Outline
Part One

Pau. Prep. & Meth.

I. **Je.** 1. Train. fai. 2. Part in Syn.

II. **Trai. Rec. Rab.** Sch. of Gam.

III. **Hell.** "Gre. J." Trav. Gre. Lang.

IV. **Rom. cit.**

V. **Apos.**

VI. **Nat. Endow.** 1. Sym. 2. Pre. 3. Theol. 4. Tac. 5. Nat. lead. 6. Tir. Work.

Review Questions

Part One

What prominence does the book of Acts give to Paul in the period of the church among the Gentiles? How do we know that there were other workers at that time? Name some of these other workers. What churches are named which could not have been founded by Paul? What was Paul's age at the opening of this period? What were some advantages which Paul possessed for his work? What were the advantages of his birth and training as a Jew? What education did he receive, and wherein was it a help to him? To what great branch of the Jews did Paul belong? How was this fact an advantage in his work? Of what nation was he a citizen? Name instances when this fact was of avail to Paul. With what authority could Paul speak? Whence came this authority? What were some of Paul's natural endowments for his ministry? What does Paul mean by the expression, "my gospel"? What showed his industry as a worker?

Part Two

VII. We must also study Paul's **Methods of Work**. These were varied greatly according to circumstances, but in them we may note certain principles.

1. *He took fellow workers* with him. Notice his companions on his first journey. Acts 13. 2-5. On his second journey. Acts 15. 40; 16. 1-3. What other companion is indicated in the word "we" in Acts 16. 10? On his third journey. Acts 19. 22, 29. Other companions on this journey. Acts 20. 4, 5. This method gave 1.) *Mutual encouragement*. Paul was social, loved companionship; was sometimes melancholy when alone (Acts 17.

15, 16; 2 Cor. 2. 12, 13; 2 Cor. 7. 5, 6). 2.) *Power in co-operation*; two can do much more than twice as much as one. 3.) There was also *training* for younger workers, whom Paul always took with him; e. g., Mark, Timothy, and perhaps Titus.

2. *He chose the cities*; and of these the largest and most important centers of population. Antioch, Thessalonica, Corinth, Ephesus, Rome. Paul was, in training and tastes, a man of the city, not of the country. He took great interest in men, but apparently none in nature. Contrast Paul in this respect with Christ, most of whose illustrations were drawn from nature. One result of Paul's choice of the cities was the wide and rapid diffusion of the gospel. The cities became Christian long before the country-places. The word "pagan" literally means "countryman," but it came to mean a worshiper of idols. See the effect of Paul's two years in Ephesus (Acts 19. 10). "The seven churches of Asia" (Rev. 1. 11) were the outgrowth of Paul's work in Ephesus.

3. *He supported himself by his trade.* His occupation. Acts 18. 3. References to his self-support in different places. 1 Cor. 4. 12; 1 Thess. 2. 9; Acts 20. 34; Paul's was a "self-supporting mission," because there was no society to support him and he would not lay the burden upon those just converted. But although he asked no contributions, he accepted them when tendered. Phil. 4. 15; 16. 18.

4. *He began in the synagogue.* In every large city there were Jewish synagogues; and in these Paul could speak as an accepted Rabbi. Note how constantly he made use of the synagogue. Acts 13. 4, 5. Acts 14. 1. Acts 17. 1. Acts 18. 4, 19. This method gave him access to the worshiping Scripture-loving *Jews*, to whom he felt called to give the gospel first (Rom. 1. 16). But it also gave him access to the thoughtful, serious *Gentiles* who were seeking after God; and from this class came many of the early Christians. Notice that in Paul's opening address in Antioch in Pisidia he addressed both these classes (Acts 13. 16). The synagogue among the Jews of the dispersion was a great aid to the gospel.

5. He formed *acquaintance with rulers* and influential men in many places; in so many that it cannot have been accidental, but must have been a part of his plan. Examine the following references, and note names and places: Acts 13. 7. Acts 17. 34. Rom. 16. 23. Acts 19. 31. Acts 28. 7. These friendships were often of great service to Paul, especially when opposed by his own people.

6. *He used the pen* as well as the voice. He wrote many letters, not so much to spread the gospel as to strengthen and instruct the churches

which he had planted. A number of his letters to churches and to individuals have been preserved; but it is evident that some have been lost (1 Cor. 5. 9. Col. 4. 16).

7. He strengthened his work by frequently *revisiting his churches.* Notice a re-visitation on his first journey (Acts 14. 21). The same churches visited again on his second journey (Acts 16. 1-4). Again on his third journey he passed through the same places (Acts 19. 1). A re-visitation of the European churches (Acts 20. 1, 2).

VIII. Note, lastly, **Paul's Enemies**; those who throughout his journeys opposed, fought, persecuted him. Almost everywhere his work stirred up violent antagonisms. This came in different places from three sources:

1. *The Jews*, whose opposition came not so much from his preaching Jesus as the Messiah as from his willingness to receive Gentiles into the church. He was regarded as breaking down the distinctions between Jew and Gentile. Note instances of persecution from this source (Acts 13. 45, 50. Acts 14. 1, 2. Acts 14. 19. Acts 17. 5. Acts 21. 27).

2. *The Judaizing Christians*; professed disciples who were opposed to Gentile membership in the church (Acts 15. 1, 5. Acts 21. 20, 21. Phil. 1. 14-17). As the years passed the proportion of Jews to Gentiles in the church became less and less, and this party diminished in power.

3. *The Gentiles.* In only two places do we find persecution stirred up against Paul by Gentiles without suggestion by Jews. Note the places and circumstances in Acts 16. 16-24. Acts 19 23-30. In each instance private interests caused the trouble. As yet there was no strife between Christianity and the imperial government. But Paul saw the trials impending, and not far distant, and he forewarned his churches of sharper persecution soon to come (Thess. 2. 3-10. Acts 20. 29. Phil. 1. 28-30).

Blackboard Outline

Part Two

VII **Pau. Meth. Wor.** 1. Fell. work. 2. Ch. cit. 3. Sup. by tra. 4. Beg. . syn. 5. Acq. w. ral. 6. Us. pen. 7. Rev. chu.

VIII. **Pau. Ene.** 1. Je. 2. Jud. Chr. 3. Gen.

Review Questions. Part Two

Name seven facts about Paul's methods of work in the gospel. Who were his companions on his first, second, and third journeys? What were the benefits of having fellow-workers? Name some cities where Paul labored longest. How is Paul contrasted in this respect with Jesus Christ? What was the effect of beginning the work in the great cities? How was Paul supported while preaching? Why did he follow that plan? In what place did Paul begin his work wherever possible? Whom did he reach in that method? Name some rulers and influential people in different places who were friends of Paul. What use of the pen did Paul make in his ministry? Show how he frequently revisited his churches. What three classes of people were enemies of Paul in his work? Name instances when the Jews opposed him. What was their reason for their opposition? What opposition did he meet from fellow-Christians? At what places was he persecuted by Gentiles? What was the attitude of the Roman government at that time toward Christianity?

SEVENTEENTH STUDY

The Church among the Gentiles

From the Council at Jerusalem, A. D. 50, To the Death of St. Paul, A. D. 68.

Part One

The history of this period of eighteen years, as contained in the book of Acts, is limited to the labors of St. Paul, who was pre-eminently the apostle to the Gentiles (2 Tim. 1. 11).

I. Let us draw the **map of the lands** embraced in the later journeys of the apostle Paul.

1. *The Lands*: 1.) Asia Minor. 2.) Thrace. 3.) Macedonia. 4.) Greece or Achaia. 5.) Italy. 6.) Africa, not visited by Paul. 7.) Palestine or Judea. 8.) Syria.

2. *The Localities.* 1.) Jerusalem. 2.) Antioch. 3.) Ephesus. 4.) Troas. 5.) Philippi. 6.) Thessalonica. 7.) Berea. 8.) Athens. 9.) Corinth. 10.) Rome.

II. **Paul's Second Missionary Journey.** The gospel in Europe (A. D. 51-53). Notice:

1. *His companions*: the quarrel with Barnabas and separation (Acts 15. 36-39). Barnabas at this point drops out of the record. Silas, Timothy, and later Luke, accompany Paul (Acts 15. 40; 16. 1; 16. 10). Luke's profession, perhaps therein helping the apostle (Col. 4. 14).

2. *Asia Minor revisited.* Note and locate the provinces through which they passed, starting from Antioch: 1.) Cilicia (Acts 15. 41). 2.) Lycaonia (Acts 16. 1, 3.) Probably Pisidia (Acts 16. 4). 4.) Galatia. 5.) Phrygia

(Acts 16. 6). Through Mysia to Troas (Acts 16. 8). Locate these provinces on the map.

3. *The Gospel in Europe.* Note the events which led to the voyage across the Ægean Sea (Acts 16. 9). Trace the route on the map—from what city? to what city? The three cities in Macedonia (Acts 16. 12; 17. 1; 17. 10). The two cities in Greece (Acts 17. 15; 18. 1). Note the long stay in Corinth (Acts 18. 11); the largest city in Greece and the commercial metropolis, at that time far more important than Athens.

Review and locate the five cities in Europe thus far visited, P. T. B. A. C., and recall the peculiar events at each place.

4. *The two Epistles to the Thessalonians* were written while Paul was at Corinth, perhaps 52 and 53 A. D. These are the earliest extant writings of Paul, and the earliest books of the New Testament. Two subjects are presented in both letters: 1.) General precepts concerning *Christian character*. 2.) The *second coming of Christ*.

5. *A visit to Ephesus*, the chief city of Asia Minor (Acts 18. 18, 19). Notice what would be the direct route from Corinth. Paul's stay at this time was short, but with promise of a speedy return.

6. *Return to Antioch.* The route, from Ephesus to Cæsarea, thence to the mother church at Jerusalem, thence 250 miles either by land via Damascus, or by water via Cæsarea (Acts 18. 22). The great result of the second missionary journey was the planting of the gospel in Europe. The churches founded were composed of both Jews and Gentiles, with the latter largely in the majority.

Blackboard Outline
Part One

I **Map.** 1. Lands. 1.) A. M. 2.) Th. 3.) Mac. 4.) Gre. 5.) It. 6.) Af. 7.) . Pal. 8.) Syr.

2. **Pla.** 1.) Jer. 2.) Ant. 3.) Eph. 4.) Tro. 5.) Phi. 6.) Thes. 7.) Ber. 8.) Ath. 9.) Cor.

I.
Pau. Sec. Miss. Jour. 1. Comp. S. T. L.

2. *As. Min. Rev.* 1.) Cil. 2.) Ly. 3.) Pi. 4.) Gal. 5.) Ph. 6.) My. T.

3. *Gos. in Eur.* Tro. Phil. Thess. Ber. Ath. Cor.

4. *Ep. Thess.* 1.) Chr. Char. 2.) Chr. sec. com.

5. *Vis. Eph.*

6. *Ret. Ant.* Result-Gosp. Eur.

Review Questions. Part One

What lands in Asia are named with this lesson on the map? What lands in Europe? What localities in Palestine and Syria? Localities in Asia Minor? Localities in Europe? Who were Paul's companions on his second missionary journey? What places of his earlier journey were revisited at this time? What new places did he visit in Asia Minor? What event called Paul to go to Europe? In what city in Europe did Paul first preach the gospel? How was his work in that city interrupted? What other places in Macedonia did he visit? In which of these places did he find the people "more noble"? What cities in Greece did he visit? In which city did he stay for a long time, and for what reason? What letters were written during this journey? From what place was each written? What was the subject or purpose of each epistle? What large city in Asia Minor was the last one visited on this journey? At what places did Paul stop on his return journey? Where did his journey end? What was the great result of this journey?

Part Two

II. **Paul's Third Missionary Journey** (A. D. 54-58). His companions are named in Acts 19. 22. The latter seems to have been a man of importance from Corinth (Rom. 16. 23). We trace the journey, starting, as both the former journeys, from Antioch:

1. *From Antioch to Ephesus* (Acts 18. 23). He went through Galatia and Phrygia, visiting churches already founded. Some think that this indicates a fourth visit to Lycaonia and Pisidia, as those lands were loosely regarded as belonging to Galatia; but this is not certain.

2. *Three years in Ephesus.* (Acts 19. 1-20.) In this metropolis of Asia Minor Paul made a stay longer than in any other place during his ministry. As results, churches arose in all that region: Colossæ (Col. 2. 2; 2. 1), Hierapolis (Col. 4. 13), and "the seven churches of Asia" (Rev. 1. 11).

3. *Macedonia and Greece revisited.* We can tell what places he would visit in this journey through former fields, although they are not named— the four or five cities wherein he had already planted churches: Philippi, Thessalonica, Berea (Athens?), Corinth. One of his errands on this journey, not mentioned in Acts, is frequently referred to in the epistles of this period, his *collection for the poor Christians in Judea.* See Rom. 15. 26, 27. 1 Cor. 16. 1-3. 2 Cor. 9. 1-4. Probably the care of these funds was one reason for the large number of disciples accompanying Paul on his return journey (Acts 20. 4).

4. *Epistles of this Period.* These were the following:

1.) *First Corinthians*, written from Ephesus, perhaps about 57 A. D. Its occasion (1 Cor. 1. 11, 12). Its purpose, to set forth a true church-life.

2.) *Second Corinthians* (57 A. D.), probably written from Macedonia. (2 Cor. 7. 5; 8. 1); its purpose, mainly a defense of Paul's apostolic authority.

3.) *Galatians*, also probably from Macedonia (57 A. D). Its occasion, the influence of Judaizing teachers on Paul's churches in Galatia (Gal. 1. 6, 7). "Galatia" may refer to the regions in Lycaonia and Pisidia (according to Ramsay); but most expositors refer it to Galatia Proper, north of those provinces. The theme of this book is "Salvation by faith *only*."

4.) *Romans* was written from Corinth perhaps in 58 A. D. See Rom. 16. 1, a reference to the seaport of Corinth. Its subject is "Justification by Faith." Notice how important were the writings of this period.

5. *The return journey* (Acts 20. 6-21, 17). Note the route and places, which should be traced on the map. 1.) Philippi (Acts 20. 6). 2.) Troas (Acts 20. 6-13). What took place at Troas? 3.) Voyage to Miletus (Acts 20. 14, 15). 4.) At Miletus, a touching address (Acts 20. 17-38). 5.) Voyage to Tyre (Acts 21. 1-6). 6.) Ptolemais (Acts 21. 7). 7.) Cæsarea (Acts 21. 8-15.) A remarkable meeting. 8.) Jerusalem (Acts 21. 17). Paul's errand to Jerusalem was to present the contribution of the Gentile churches; seeking to reconcile them with the mother church in Jerusalem, which was exceedingly bigoted in its zeal for the law (Acts 21. 20, 21).

6. **Paul's arrest and imprisonment** (Acts 21. 27-34). Our purpose is not to narrate the personal life of St. Paul but to show the development of the Christian church, therefore we do not enter into the details of his experience. He was arrested in Jerusalem, and placed in the castle of Antonia for his protection (Acts 21. 24); subsequently taken to Cæsarea (Acts 23. 25-35). Here he remained in prison two years (Acts 24. 27). During this time Paul was placed on trial at least four times: 1.) Before the Jewish council of the Sanhedrim. (Acts 23. 1-10.) 2.) Before the Roman governor or procurator Felix. (Acts 24:. 1-22.) 3.) Before Festus, the successor of Felix. (Acts 25. 1-12.) 4.) Before Agrippa, the ethnarch of the Bashan district, called by courtesy "King Agrippa." (Acts 26. 1-32.)

Blackboard Outline
Part Two

II. **Pau. Thir. Miss. Jour.** (54-58). Comp. Tim. Eras.

1. *Ant. to Eph.* Gal. Phr.

2. *Thr. Ye. Eph.* Res. Col. Hier. "Sev. Ch. As."

3. *Mac. Gre. Rev.* Phil. Thes. Ber. (Ath.?) Cor. Coll. for Jud.

4. *Ep. Per. auth.* 1.) 1 Cor. Eph. 57. Tr. Ch. Lif. 2.) 2 Cor. 57. Mac. P. ap. 3.) Gal. Mac. 57. "Jud. tea." "Salv. fai. on." 4.) Rom. Cor. 58. "Jus. by fai."

5. *Ret. Jour.* 1.) Ph. 2.) Tro. 3.) Voy. Mil. 4.) Mil. 5.) Voy. Tyr. 6.) Ptol. 7.) Cæs. 8.) Jer.

6. *Pau. Arr. & Imp.* Jer. Cæs.

Review Questions, Part Two

Who were companions of Paul on his third journey? From what city did he start? Through what lands did he first pass? What great city was his principal field of labor? In what neighboring cities did churches arise as a result? What provinces in Europe, and what cities in them, did he revisit? What was one of his important errands on this journey? Who accompanied Paul on his return? What letters were written while Paul was on this journey? Name the place from which each of these epistles was written. State the approximate date of each letter. What was the purpose or theme of each letter? Name some of the places where Paul stopped on his return journey. What took place at Troas? What took place at Miletus? Whom did Paul meet at Cæsarea? What was Paul's destination? What was his purpose in visiting the mother church? What happened to Paul at Jerusalem? To what place was he afterwards taken? How long was he a prisoner in that place?

Part Three

IV. **Paul's Fourth Journey** (Acts 27 and 28). Although made by a prisoner, some of the time wearing a chain (Acts 26. 29; 28. 20), the journey to Rome was a missionary journey, in many respects like Paul's other journeys. To visit Rome had long been his desire and expectation (Acts 19. 21. Rom. 1. 15. Rom. 15. 23, 24). His companions on the journey, Luke, Aristarchus (Acts 27. 1, 2), and probably Timothy.

1. On the voyage he was able to bring the *gospel to the island of Malta* (Acts 28. 7-10).

2. Arriving at *Rome* (Acts 28. 16) he took up his work as nearly as possible according to his *regular method*. 1.) He found a *home* and *employment* (Acts 28. 16). 2.) As he could not go to the synagogue he *sent for the chief Jews* and preached the gospel to them (Acts 28. 17-24). 3.) He then turned to the Gentiles (Acts 28. 28-31). 4.) Some *results* of his ministry in Rome (Phil 1. 12-18).

3. *The Epistles of Paul's Imprisonment at Rome.* The order of these is uncertain, but they belong rather to the close of the period than to its opening.

1.) *Ephesians*; called by S. T. Coleridge "the divinest composition of man;" written A. D. 62; its subject, "The mystical union of Christ and his church."

2.) *Philippians*; the most affectionate of all Paul's letters; written A. D. 62; its subject "The character of Christ's followers."

3.) *Colossians*; written to a church that Paul had never seen; about A. D. 62; subject, "Christ the Head of the Church."

4.) *Philemon*: a personal letter to a friend at Colossæ concerning a *runaway slave* Onesimus, whom Paul sent back, "no longer a slave, but a brother beloved."

V. **Paul's Later Years.** The record is uncertain, and almost unknown. It is probable, though not certain, that Paul was set free about 63 A. D.

1. *His years of liberty.* 63 to 67 A. D. Shall we speak of a *fifth journey*? We find hints or expectations of his being at Colossæ (Philem. 22); Miletus (2 Tim. 4. 13); Nicopolis, north of Greece, on the Adriatic Sea (Titus 3. 12). Tradition states that at this place he was arrested, and sent from it a second time to Rome.

2. *His last epistles.* It is not certain that all the "pastoral epistles" were written by Paul. 1.) They are unlike his other writings in their style. 2.) His doctrinal views are not prominent in them. Yet on the whole, they show a reasonable probability of Paul's authorship.

1.) *First Timothy* was written during the period of liberty, between 63 and 66 A. D., as a book of *counsels to a minister*, Timothy, in charge of the church at Ephesus.

2.) *Titus*, about the same time and for the same purpose; to Titus, in charge of churches on the island of Crete.

3.) *Second Timothy*, from Rome, during Paul's second and last imprisonment; a letter of farewell counsels to his "son Timothy." Strictly speaking this book should be named under the next subject.

VI. **The First Imperial Persecution.** The Christians were becoming numerous in Rome, as well as throughout the empire; and a conflict was sure to arise with the Roman government. The first persecution came soon after the burning of Rome, A. D. 64, which Nero charged falsely upon the Christians. Thousands were put to death, although the persecution was mainly limited to the capital. The *martyrdom of St. Paul*, probably of St. Peter also, took place about 68 A. D. at Rome.

Blackboard Outline
Part Three

IV. **Pau. Fou. Jour.** Pris. Comp. Lu. Aris. Tim.

1. Gos. Mal.

2. Ro. 1.) Ho. Emp. 2.) Sent. Ch. Je. 3.) Tur. Gen. 4.) Res. min.

3. Ep. Pau. Imp. 1.) Eph. "Mys. Un. Ch. and Ch." 2.) Phil. "Char. Chr. fol."   3.) Col. "Chr. Hea. Ch."   4.) Philem. Run. Sla.

V. **Pau. Lat. Ye.** 1. Yea. Lib. Col. Mil. Nicop. 2. Las. Ep. 1.) 1 Tim. 2.) Tit. 3.) 2 Tim.

VI. **Fir. Imp. Per.** Mart. Pau. 68 A. D.

Review Questions. Part Three

Under what circumstances did Paul make his fourth journey? Who were his companions? Where did he preach the gospel on his journey? How did he follow his regular method, as far as possible, at Rome? What were some results of his ministry in Rome? What epistles were written at Rome? What is the subject of these epistles? How long was Paul at liberty after his first imprisonment? What places did he probably visit during those years? What were the last three epistles written by Paul? What is the subject of each epistle? How did the first imperial persecution of the Christians arise? Who probably suffered martyrdom at this time?

EIGHTEENTH STUDY

The End of the Age

From the Death of St. Paul, A. D. 68, to the Death of St. John, 100 A. D.

Part One

We come now to our last period, an *age of shadows*, of which we know very little, and wish that we knew more. The curtain of New Testament history falls while St. Paul is still a prisoner at Rome, five years before the supposed date of his death. From that time, A. D. 63, to about A. D. 125 there is very little history, and none in the New Testament; we are left to hints, traditions, and conjectures.

A question which we would like to answer is, What became of the *companions* of St. Paul: such men as Timothy (Heb. 13. 23), Titus (2 Tim. 4. 10), Apollos (Titus 3. 13), Luke (2 Tim. 4. 11)? All of these were living and working at the close of Paul's life; but there is no report of their life and labors after that event.

Another perplexing fact is that when the curtain rises at about 125 A. D. it shows us a very *different church* from that of St. Paul's day: a church completely organized, with bishops in almost absolute control; and sects quarreling over controversies apparently unknown when St. Paul wrote his letters.

While Peter and Paul were living the church had wise and statesmanlike leaders, who directed its energies. But when these great men died "second-rate men" were left in control and they were not equal to the demand of the new time; and the church drifted into disputes, which grew into divisions. Let us notice the few known **Events of this Period**.

I. **The Fall of Jerusalem**: epoch-making, not only to Jewish but also to Christian history.

1. The *rebellion of the Jews* against the Roman power began in 68 A. D.; hopeless from the beginning—for how could one small state measure swords with the empire of the civilized world? The city of Jerusalem was taken and destroyed 70 A. D , and with it fell forever the Jewish state.

2. The *siege had been predicted* in the gospels (Matt. 24. 15-18; Mark 13. 14), and was expected by the disciples of Christ. The *Christians* in Jerusalem and Judea *withdrew* to *Pella* in the Jordan valley; but their numbers were not large, showing that Jewish Christianity must have declined since A. D. 58 (see Acts 21. 20), while Gentile Christianity had increased. After the destruction of Jerusalem Jewish Christianity

remained for 200 years a feeble and declining sect, hated by their own people as traitors, and despised by Gentile Christians because they still observed the Jewish law.

3. The effect of the fall of Jerusalem was to draw a sharp line of *division between Jews and Christians*. Before, the two classes had been closely related, and confused in the popular mind. Thenceforth the two streams ran further and further apart, and have continued apart even to our own time. All Jewish rites ceased in the church, Christians could no longer be Jews; and after 125 A. D. Jews could no longer be Christians without renouncing Judaism. The church was now thoroughly a Gentile, non-Jewish church. Note in the gospel of John how "the Jews" are everywhere named as enemies of Christ (John 5. 16; 7. 1; 11. 8; 18. 36); and yet the author of this book was himself a Jew by birth and training; but at the time of writing he had ceased to be a Jew.

II. **St. John at Ephesus.** Ephesus, at the western end of Asia Minor, was now the leading city of Christianity. It is probable that the apostle John passed the last thirty years of his life in that city. He was revered as the *last of the apostles*; but he was not a statesman or man of affairs; rather a mystic and man of meditation. It is supposed that he died about 100 A. D. but the date is not certain.

III. **The Rise of the Heresies.** 1. This was the inevitable *result of the Greek mind* working on the simple doctrines of the gospel. The Christian doctrine was Jewish; and the Jewish mind was not given to subtle intellectual questions. But when Christianity ceased to be Jewish and began to Gentile it was dominated by the Greek spirit of restless inquiry. Asia Minor was the home of wild, uncontrolled thinking. Sects almost without number appeared, wrangled, and divided over every article of the creed. The more mysterious the question, the more apart from practical life and from human interest, the more fascinating became the study.

2. Two great classes of sects embraced many minor groups.

1.) *The Ebionites.* Strict Jews, who sought to make Christianity a branch of Pharisaism, keeping the Jewish law. 2.) *The Gnostics.* People with peculiar views concerning the nature of God, heavenly beings, the nature of Christ.

3. The *results* of these controversies were both good and evil. 1.) *Good* in that the clashing of ideas aided in *fixing* in permanent form the true *doctrines* of the church. 2.) But far more *evil*; for the energies of the members were absorbed in debate and controversy; the spiritual life of the church greatly declined; the aim ceased to be devotion to Christ, but

was now orthodoxy in belief. Christianity became a creed, instead of an inner spiritual life.

IV. **The Second Imperial Persecution**; under the emperor Domitian, son of Titus, about A. D. 95. This was far more widely extended than the former persecution under Nero; and it was followed by a long series of persecutions, wherein untold thousands of Christians were put to death. The inevitable conflict had come between Christianity and the Roman empire, and it lasted two hundred years; but at its close the cross was triumphant over the Roman eagles. It is not difficult to see the *causes* of this *struggle*:

1. *Heathenism was hospitable*, welcoming new gods and goddesses, while *Christianity was exclusive*, opposing with all its might every other form of worship.

2. *Idol-worship* and its services were *interwoven* with all the *life of the people*; personal, family, social, political. Temples, statues, festivals were constantly in evidence; on all occasions there were rites of worship. But here was a growing multitude of people who stood aloof from these exercises. It was not strange that these people were regarded as enemies of society and of the state.

3. Certain forms of religion were allowed in the Roman empire, but all new forms were forbidden. *Judaism was a permitted* religion. As long as Christianity was looked upon as a branch of Judaism, it was allowed. But after the fall of Jerusalem it stood alone, an unlicensed form of worship, hence under suspicion; suspicion readily becoming enmity.

4. *The worship of the emperor* was the one most prevalent throughout the empire. A statue of the reigning emperor stood in every city, and it was a test of loyalty to offer libations of incense before it. This worship is doubtless referred to in an enigmatic manner in such passages as 2 Thess. 2. 3, 4. Rev. 13. 1, 4, 8, 18. This worship was refused by the Christians, who were for that reason regarded as disloyal.

From these causes persecution after persecution arose; hundreds of thousands perished; yet in spite of the persecution, the church grew rapidly.

Blackboard Outline
Part One

    En. Ag. Ag. shad. Comp. Paul. Diff. Ch. 125 A. D. "Sec. ra. m."

I. **Fa. Jer.** 1.) Reb. A. D. 68-70. 2.) Siege pred. Chr. with. Pel. 3.) Eff. div. Je. Chr.

II **Jhn. Eph.** Last. Ap. 100 A. D.

II
I. **Ris. Her.** 1. Gre. min. 2. Eb. Gnos. 3. Res. 1.) G. 2.) Ev.

I **Sec. Imp. Per.** Dom. 95. Caus. 1. Heath. hosp. 2. Id. wor. int. li. 3. V. Jud. per. rel. Chr. unlic. 4. Wor. Emp.

Review Questions

What is said of the period after the death of St. Paul? Between what years is there very little history? What companions of St. Paul were living at the time of his death? What became of these men? Wherein was the church of a later period different from that of the earlier time? What reason is assigned for these changes? Name the four principal events in the period under consideration. When did the rebellion of the Jews against the Roman empire begin? What was the result of this rebellion? What became of the Christians in Jerusalem at the opening of the Jewish war? What was the after history of Jewish Christianity? What was the effect of the fall of Jerusalem on the relations between Christianity and Judaism? Who was the last of the twelve apostles on the earth? Where did he live? What was his character? What is said as to his death? What divisions in the church arose at this period? Of what were these divisions the result? What country was the home of the heresies? Who were the Ebionites? Who were the Gnostics? What good result came from these controversies? What evil result followed them? What persecution arose during this period? At what time? Under what emperor did the persecution begin? How did it compare with the earlier persecution under Nero? What general causes may be given for the series of imperial persecutions of the Christians? Wherein was heathenism hospitable, and Christianity exclusive? How was idolatry interwoven with the affairs of life? How was this fact adverse to the Christians? How did Christianity come to be looked on with suspicion in the empire? How did the worship of the emperor affect the Christians? What is this worship called in the New Testament? Did these persecutions stop the progress of the church?

Part Two

Let us consider the **condition of the church** at the end of the first century, seventy years after the Ascension of our Lord.

I. **Its Numbers** cannot be definitely stated; but the church was very large, and growing with marvelous rapidity. Sources of information: 1.) *The catacombs*; cemeteries under and around Rome where Christians only were buried, and wherein they met in times of persecution; occupied between 100 and 400 A. D.; containing in three centuries two million graves of Christians. 2.) A letter of Pliny, Roman governor of Bithynia-

Pontus in Asia Minor, 112 A. D., stating that "the temples were almost deserted," "an incredible number of professors." Evidences point to the church, A. D. 100, having already a large proportion of the population of the Roman empire.

II. **Its Membership.** 1. Once the church had been entirely Jewish; then it became Jewish and Gentile; now it was almost everywhere a Gentile church, with a few Jewish members, most of whom had abandoned Jewish rites and rules and were regarded by the Jews as "apostates."

2. *Its social condition* was varied. It is a mistake to suppose that at any time the early church was composed mainly of slaves and the poorest classes. Such there were; but there were also men of wealth, of high rank, and of great influence. There is reason to believe that some relatives of the emperor, previous to 100 A. D. were banished on account of their Christian profession. The gospel had by this time permeated all classes.

III. **Its Organization.** We observe in this respect a remarkable change since the period of St. Paul's ministry. Everywhere the church was hardening into an *ecclesiastical system ruled by bishops*. Bishops are first mentioned late in St. Paul's ministry (Acts 20. 28; Rev. Ver. Phil. 1. 1; 1 Tim. 3. 1-7); but it is evident that the word at that time meant no more than "elder;" otherwise the elders of Ephesus would not have been called "bishops" in Acts 20.28. But in an autocratic state the church would naturally become autocratic in its arrangement, ruled from above rather than from below. By 125 A. D. bishops were in control everywhere.

IV. **Its Institutions.** Two of these require notice. 1. *The Lord's Supper.* We have seen how this began as a service in the home, like the Jewish Passover, out of which it grew (Acts 2. 46). But among Gentile churches the custom arose of celebrating it at a public meeting, as a supper to which each member brought some share of provision. See 1 Cor. 11. 20-30, an account of abuses that had arisen. By the end of the first century the supper had become a service held at the meeting place of the Christians, but not in public. All except members of the church were excluded from this service, which was held as a "mystery."

2. *The Lord's Day.* The observance of the first day of the week grew gradually, and with its growth the recognition of the Jewish sabbath declined. Note the development indicated in 1 Cor. 16. 2; Acts 20. 7; Rev. 1. 10. As the church became entirely a Gentile institution "the Lord's day" took the place of the Jewish sabbath.

V. **Its Doctrinal System.** The *theology of St. Paul*, as set forth in Romans and Ephesians, was now accepted as the doctrine of the church.

Notice that St. Peter (1 Pet. 1. 18-21) states the great Pauline principle of justification by faith through the blood of Christ.

VI. Its Literature. By 100 A. D. all the books of the New Testament were written, though not all of them were everywhere accepted as authoritative. In some places there were questions about Hebrews, 2 Peter and Revelation; the latter because local in its address, and so recent in origin as not to be known everywhere. But the gospels (except John, which was about 95 A. D. in its date), the Acts and nearly all the epistles were read in all the churches as possessing an inspired authority. Note that, in 2 Peter, Paul's writings are placed on a par with "the other Scriptures," which must refer to the Old Testament.

VII. Its Spiritual Life. It must be admitted that there had been a decline in the fervency of the Christian life in the church. Its moral standards were still high; but spiritual gifts had become less noticeable; the rule of bishops and councils and the controversies over doctrines were weakening the fervor of spirituality. Note the difference in spirit and tone between the writings of the New Testament and those of the early church-fathers in the second century.

Blackboard Outline
Part Two

    Cond. of Ch. 100 A. D.

I. **Num.** 1.) Cat. 2.) Let. Plin.

II. **Mem.** 1.) Gen. few Je. 2.) Soc. cond. all class.

III. **Org.** Ecc. Sys. ru. b. Bish.

IV. **Inst.** Lor. Sup. Lor. D.

V. **Doc. Sys.** Theo. Pau.

VI. **Lit.** N. T.

VII. **Spir. Lif.** Dec.

Review Questions. Part Two

What is the estimate of the number of members in the church at the end of the first century? What evidence of this is found in the Catacombs of

Rome? What evidence is given by a letter? Who wrote this letter, and when was it written? Was the church at this time Jewish or Gentile? What was the relation of Jewish believers to the church? Of what social elements was the church composed? How was the church organized at this time? What references to "bishops" are found in the New Testament, and what do they indicate? How did the bishops grow to be rulers in the church? What two institutions of the church are referred to? How was the Lord's Supper observed in the earliest church? What changes arose in the method of administration? How did the first day of the week come to be recognized in the church? What was the doctrinal system of this time? What was the literature of the church? What books were at first questioned? What was the spiritual condition of the church as compared with earlier periods? What may have caused the decline in spiritual fervor?

The End

Made in the USA
Las Vegas, NV
27 February 2023

68247712R00056